MORE PARABLES AND FABLES

Peter Ribes SJ

more Parables and Fables

ST PAULS

Originally published by St Paul Publications, India
© St Paul Publications, Bombay

The texts in this book have been revised and adapted by Christina Bell

Cover and illustrations by Sarah John

St Pauls
Middlegreen, Slough SL3 6BT, United Kingdom
Moyglare Road, Maynooth, Co. Kildare, Ireland

© St Pauls 1993

ISBN 085439 431 1

Printed by The Guernsey Press Co. Ltd, Guernsey, C.I.

St Pauls is an activity of the priests and brothers of the Society of St Paul who proclaim the Gospel through the media of social communication

Contents

Foreword	7
Hints on how to use the parables	9
PART 1	
The cobbler	17
I can't do it, dad!	23
The holy man and the lost travellers	26
Night flight	28
The rabbi's forest, fire and prayer	32
The saviours	36
The strawberry	40
The watchman	43
The wisest of them all	40
PART 2	
A divided world	55
Dream or reality?	62
Greedy Timothy	69
Please, help me!	73

The swallow and the frogs	78
Swimmy	82
Teachers wanted	86
Things money cannot buy	90
Who killed Pat Hudson?	95
The world map jigsaw puzzle	99

PART 3

The bird and the well	103
The cuckoo	107
Princess Ugly	111
Procrustes	115
Which guide to follow?	117
The portrait	121
Tom and Sam	125
To save or not to save one's skin	128
The unbeaten road	132
The tree, the roots and the soil	137

Foreword

Dear Reader,

Three years ago I prepared a volume of *Parables and Fables for Modern Man* which was published by St Paul Publications.

My aim then was to help group moderators and animators, teachers of religion and moral science and even preachers in their ministry.

That book met with such instant success that I felt encouraged to prepare a few volumes more.

In this second volume you will find 29 parables and stories bearing mainly on 'religious, personal and social values'. I am sure that this volume will prove useful and practical too. In this volume also I have introduced some changes such as:

- To make its reading easier and more pleasurable I have changed the literary style from 'script writing' for audiovisuals and 'skit presentation' into plain 'story telling'.
- I have shortened most of the parables.
- Incase you would like to use the parables for group discussion or any other group sessions, I

have appended after each story a simple ready-made questionnaire.

– I have added after some parables, which by their nature may prove more difficult for discussion, some helpful notes and reflections.

May the good Lord bless our efforts to spread the Good News and help our brothers and sisters live meaningful lives.

Hints on how to use the parables for reflection and discussion

General ideas

Purpose of parables

Parables are not 'gap fillers' or 'time-killers' to entertain the audience. They are meant to be 'starters' or 'triggers' to provoke the participants to think, discuss and interact. They are only the beginning of a process of reflection and discussion.

Moderators

– Be quick to pick up the reactions of the group. Be sensitive to the habits and feelings of your audience.
– Accept the participants as they are. Keep going at their pace. Do not hurry! Have patience.
– Begin from where they are and gently lead them as far as possible where you would like them to go.

Ways of presentation

Present your parables in the most fascinating way you can. We suggest below some ways of presentation.
– *Read clearly* and intelligibly the parable.
– *Distribute copies* of it to all and request them to read it very attentively.
– *Narrate or retell* the parable, or have it retold by some good storyteller.
– *Have it mimed.* A few chosen participants should be prepared.
– *Have it acted in a skit form.* Previous preparation is wanted.
– Make use of puppets.
– *Use radio-play techniques.* Prepare a sount track and replay it.
– *Poster story.* Have some participants to prepare beforehand some posters. They will explain the parable to the rest by means of their posters.

Procedure

Before presentation

– Create in your audience sufficient awareness and willingness to cooperate.
– Let them know that the parable is being presented in view of a serious reflection and discussion to follow.
– Request them that while the parable is being presented they should keep questioning mentally what its meaning might be.

– Insist on attentive silence throughout the presentation. All comments are to be kept for after the presentation.

– Do not announce the title of the parable nor its contents.

After the presentation

REFLECTION AND SHARING

– Give the participants a questionnaire to help them reflect on the parable. You may use for the purpose the questionnaires or points you will find after each parable in this book. If you prefer you may prepare your own questionnaire.

It may be very useful to make the participants give their answers in writing, since in this way:

i. all, even the shy and diffident, will have something personal to share and discuss;
ii. the participants will be given a chance of deeper and more serious reflection;
iii once they have written their personal reflections they will be less likely to repeat what others have said.

– Do not be in a hurry to start the sharing of reflections. Give the group sufficient time for thinking and writing.

– As the sharing of reflections goes on the moderator or someone else will write on the blackboard the main ideas coming from the floor.

– For an orderly sharing, let all the group members share their reflections on one question at a time.

– In case the group is too large, divide them into smaller groups for sharing and the discussion to follow. Secure good animators for each group. If not available, let one of the participants act as moderator.

DISCUSSION

– After the sharing is over, identify from the items noted on the blackboard those you or the participants would like to be discussed first.

– Remember that Moderators should not manipulate or monopolise the discussion. They are only Facilitators. They should not impose their views and opinions or decide questions for the group.

– Moderators will try to get all the group members to participate – even the less vocal or the timid ones.

– An atmosphere of respect and acceptance for all and freedom should be maintained.

RECAPITULATION AND INPUT

– After the discussion the Moderators will recapitulate in an input form from the points discussed. Now, they may add their own views or any points which might have been left out by the participants.

– The input of the Moderators should not be 'preachy' or 'moralistic'.

PERSONALIZATION AND GOAL SETTING

– The participants should be encouraged to reflect in silence on the consequences and applications of what has been discussed for the improvement of their lives and attitudes.

– For the personalization the three following points

may be offered to them: ask them to put their findings in writing and take them home.

1. What insights did I get from today's reflection and discussion?

2. Am I happy being what I am or with my attitudes and values towards life? Why?

3. Is there anything I want to change in my life and attitudes? What is it? How do I intend changing it?

After the *personalization* and *goal setting* close the event with a prayer or prayer session.

Lead the participants in prayer; either privately by themselves, or in small groups or within the larger group.

PART 1

Parables on religious values

The cobbler

In a small village high in the mountains there lived a cobbler. One Christmas eve, something very strange happened to him. Was it a dream, or did it really happen? No one will ever know. While the cobbler was saying his morning prayers, he heard a stranger speaking to him:

'Peter, I have come to tell you that God is pleased with you. The Lord Jesus will visit you today in your shop.'

The cobbler was overjoyed. He dusted and cleaned and swept his shop. Although he had little money, he prepared a pot of stew so that he would have food to offer his visitor. Then he put on his best clothes and settled down to work, his heart beating in anticipation.

A woman who had a bad reputation in the village walked into his shop. Although Peter greeted her warmly, he was anxious in case the Lord Jesus should arrive while she was there. He hid his anxiety and chatted kindly with her until she was ready to leave.

Alone again and waiting for his Lord, he began to imagine what it would be like to meet him face to face. 'What will he look like? Will he exude the serenity of the Christ of the icon in my church? Will he radiate the majesty of Christ the King after whom my parish is named?' Lost in thought, he did not notice that a mother and her child were standing in the doorway.

'Good morning, Peter!'

He looked up. 'You startled me. For a moment, I thought you were somebody else. Please come in. It's lovely to see you.' Peter noticed how pale and thin the child looked. Food was scarce in the village that year. 'Come child,' he said. 'Sit down. Would you like an apple? It will do you more good than it will me.'

The child turned to her mother in excitement. 'Look, an apple,' he said, and there was a hungry gleam in his eyes. When they left the shop, the little girl was carrying a new pair of shoes under her arm as a Christmas gift.

They returned home full of happiness while the cobbler sat alone and pensive, waiting for his Lord. He muttered to himself as he worked. 'Can it be possible that the Lord will come to my house today?'

All day long, a steady stream of people visited his shop. Finally, a drunkard staggered in, shouting and laughing. 'Peter, give me some vodka. I've been drinking so much wine that I've lost the taste for it. Vodka is what I want now.'

'Come, sit down, my friend,' said Peter. 'I have no vodka, but what I have I'll share with you. I have clean water and a meal which I prepared today for a special guest. Sit down with me and we'll eat together.'

Peter and the drunkard ate their meal together. They enjoyed one another's company, each in his own way. When the drunkard left, he felt comforted and able to face life's problems with greater courage.

Time went by. Twilight gave way to darkness, and

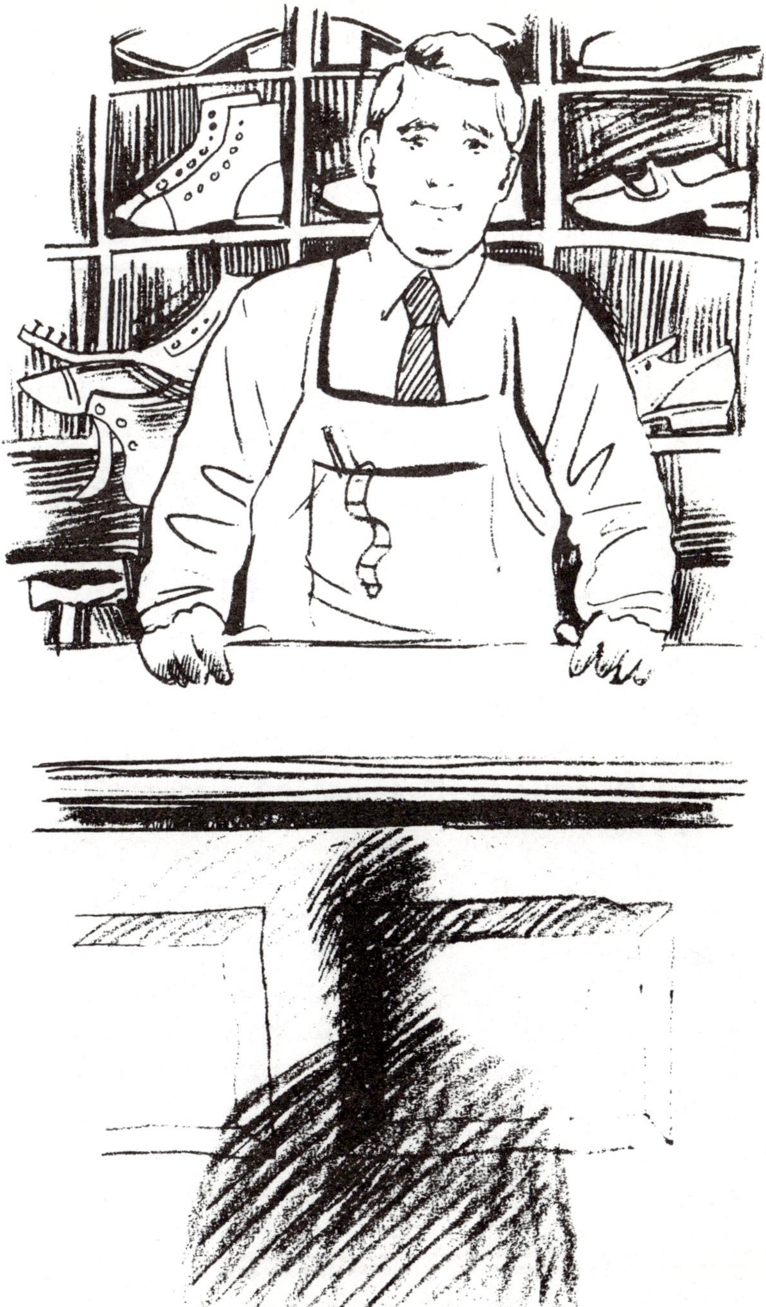

at last it was midnight. No more visitors arrived at the cobbler's shop. His spirits sank. He felt cheated and disappointed. Jesus had not come. Now it was time to go to sleep. He knelt down to say his night prayers.

'Lord, why did you not come today? I've been waiting for you all day with such eagerness.' Then he heard a voice whispering to him. 'Peter, I came to your house not just once but many times throughout the day.'

That night, Peter slept with joy and peace in his heart.

QUESTIONS FOR DISCUSSION

1. When is the best time to hear the voice of God within ourselves? Why?

2. Did Peter have good reason to feel disappointed at the end of the day?

3. Does Jesus really come into our homes today? Can you describe what he looks like?

4. Can you think of any Gospel texts which convey the same message as the story? Explain what you think they are saying.

5. In the past when Jesus came to you, how did you treat him? Are you happy with the way you entertained him?

6. Is there anything you will change in future? Can you share it with us?

POINTS FOR REFLECTION

1. If we fail to encounter Jesus in our daily lives, perhaps it is because we are failing in our encounters with other people.

2. Jesus is present in all people. If we would show him love and respect, we have to show love and respect to criminals, cheats and social misfits as much as to those we regard as decent and honest.

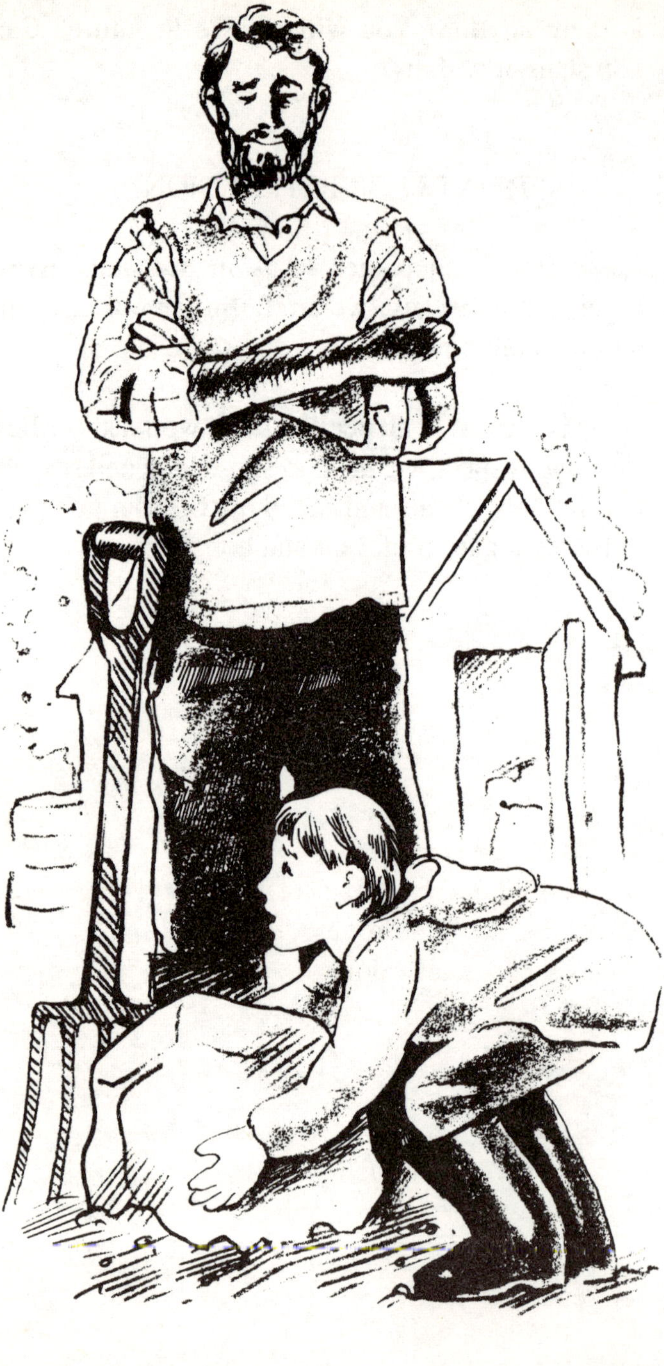

I can't do it dad!

One day, David and his father were digging a vegetable garden behind their house when they came across a large rock.

'We'll have to move this,' said his father.

'I'll move it,' said David, wanting to be helpful.

He pushed and heaved until he was breathless, but the rock wouldn't budge.

'I can't do it,' he said, admitting defeat.

'I think you can,' said his father. 'If you try everything you can think of.'

David tried again until his arms ached and he was near to tears.

'I can't do it,' he said. 'I really can't, dad. I've tried my hardest, and it hasn't moved an inch.'

'Have you really done everything you can think of?' his father asked gently. David nodded, but his father shook his head.

'No, there's one thing you've forgotten to do. If you do that, you'll be able to move the rock.'

'What have I forgotten?' David asked, puzzled. His father smiled.

'I'm right here,' he said. 'You could have asked me to help you, but you didn't.'

'Dad, will you help me?' David asked.

Father and son put their weight against the rock and they began to push. Slowly, the rock rolled away until it was clear of the vegetable garden. David laughed in delight.

'We did it, dad! We did it!' he said.

QUESTIONS FOR DISCUSSION

1. What is the value of our human efforts to attain goodness?

2. Can we accomplish salvation independently of God? Why?

POINTS FOR REFLECTION

1. We often feel that we have to carry our burdens alone, but that is not true. God is always close at hand, and he is just waiting for us to ask for his help.

2. We think that our good deeds belong only to us, but in fact they are both ours and God's, for it is he who enables us to do good.

3. God wants us to strive as if everything depended on us, and yet to trust him as if all our achievements depended on his grace and strength alone.

4. After a long night's unsuccessful fishing, Peter cast

his net on the other side of the boat at the bidding of Jesus, and then he had a large catch. But Peter still had to cast the net. Jesus did not do it for him.

The holy man
and the lost travellers

A holy man was going on a pilgrimage to a sacred shrine. The journey was difficult, and while travelling through the jungle he lost his way.

For many days, he struggled to find a way out of the jungle. He tried every path and travelled in every direction, but it was all in vain. He seemed to be moving deeper and deeper into the darkness of the forest.

Eventually, he met a group of travellers. They too were lost and were searching for the right path. When they saw the holy man they were overjoyed.

'Thanks be to God!' they said to themselves. 'This holy man will save us. He will show us the way out of the jungle.'

They began to plead with him. 'Man of God, show us the way,' they begged. 'We are lost! Help us or we will all perish.'

'I cannot tell you which path to take, because I am also looking for it,' the holy man replied. 'I can only point out the tracks which seem to lead deeper into the forest. Come, let us search together, for we are all looking for the same path. We are all looking for the path which leads to freedom and salvation.'

An Indian story

QUESTIONS FOR DISCUSSION

1. What does this story mean to you? What does it mean to others in your group?

2. Reflect on the following points and then consider the question, can anybody be sure that theirs is the only right path?

POINTS FOR REFLECTION

1. We are all wanderers in life, searching for salvation and liberation.

2. It may take much searching to discover which are the wrong paths.

3. Religious leaders and holy people, uneducated and ordinary people, are all pilgrims together.

4. No one has all the answers to life's mysteries.

5. Working together, we can help one another to discern the difference between truth and falsehood, right and wrong.

6. On our journey to God, none of us can make it alone. We have to walk together.

Night flight

One night an aeroplane was flying across the Atlantic Ocean. The passengers were enjoying dinner, soft music was playing, and the atmosphere was relaxed and peaceful. Suddenly, the plane's communication and direction-finding systems failed and the instrument panel went blank.

The flight engineer could not repair the fault. The pilot was panic-stricken. How could he reach his destination? He was flying over the ocean on a dark night with no landmarks to guide him. He asked the stewardess to find out if there was an electronics expert among the passengers.

After anxious moments, a passenger walked into the cockpit.

'Are you an electronics expert?' asked the pilot.

'No, sir,' the passenger replied. 'I know nothing at all about such things.'

'Then what are you doing in here?' asked the pilot.

'Tell me what the problem is. I may be able to help,' said the passenger.

The pilot shouted angrily. 'If you don't know anything about electronics, get out of the cockpit. You're of no use to me!'

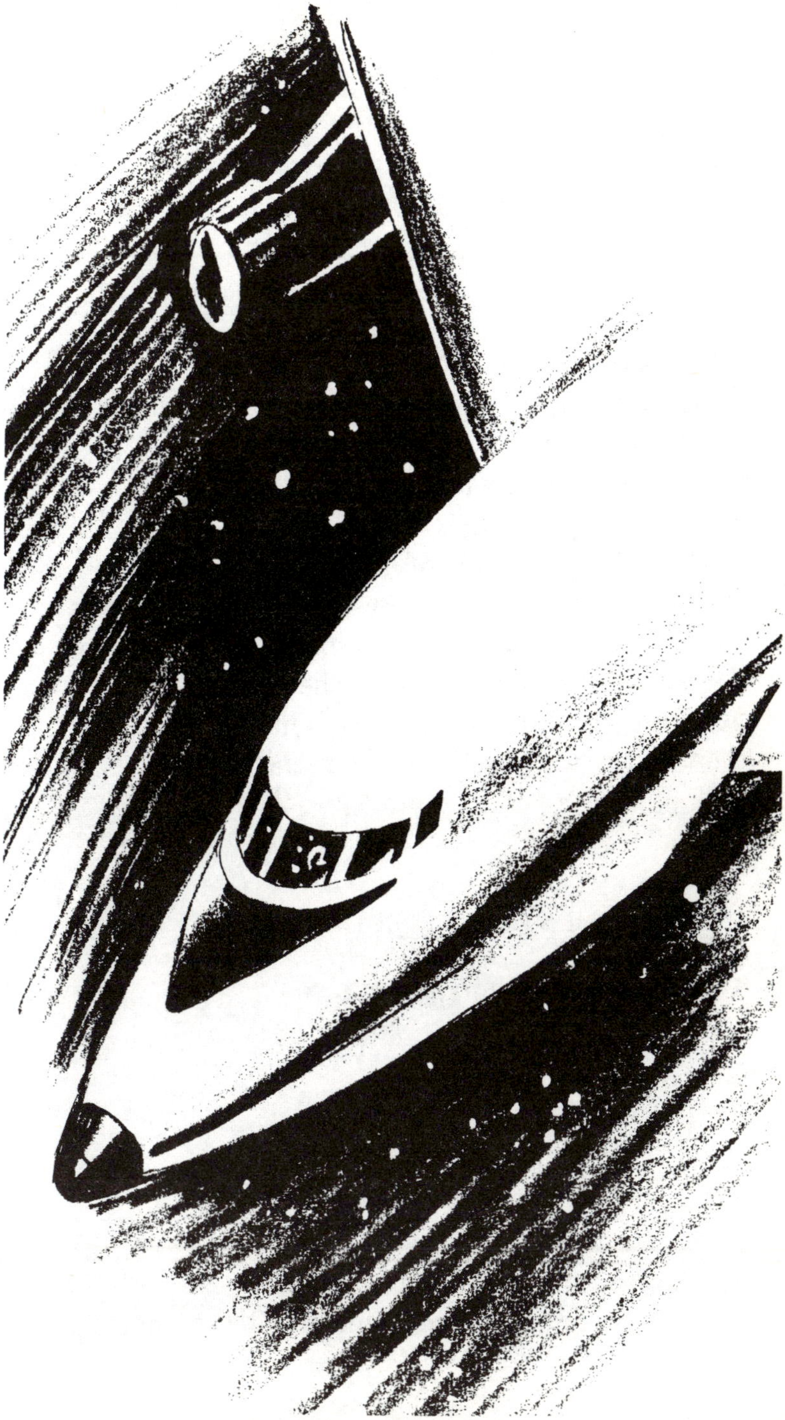

The passenger spoke quietly and politely. 'Please, tell me what the problem is. I think I can help you.'

'Can't you see for yourself?' blurted out the pilot. 'All our instrumentation has stopped working. We don't know where we are. We're lost over the ocean in the middle of the night.'

'Ah, but I *can* help you,' said the passenger. 'I know of something which never fails. It has never failed in the past, and it will never fail in the future.'

The pilot stared in disbelief. 'What are you talking about?' he asked.

'The heavens, my friend,' the stranger replied. 'The stars will be our guide. Show me your route map over the ocean and our point of destination.'

The passenger, an ordinary-looking woman, was an astronomer. She sat beside the pilot with the map on her lap and her eyes glued to the heavens. Steadily and skillfully, she directed the pilot on his flight.

At dawn, the plane landed on schedule at its destination.

QUESTIONS FOR DISCUSSION

1. What does this story mean to you?

2. Can we rely on technology and material goods to solve all the problems of human existence?

POINTS FOR REFLECTION

1. From birth to death we are on a flight over the darkness of the ocean. Guided by the shining stars

of hope, peace and love, we are travelling towards our heavenly destination, the Kingdom of God.

2. Scientists and technicians alone do not hold the key to our salvation. We also need the people of God, saintly people who study the heavens and contemplate divine realities.

3. To reach our destination we have to raise our eyes above earthly realities and consult heavenly signs. We have to pray.

4. As long as we keep looking at God, we will never lack guidance and direction in life.

The rabbi's forest, fire and prayer

An old Jewish story tells that when a calamity was threatening his people, Rabbi Israel Bell Shem-Tov used to go to a certain holy place in the forest, light a sacred fire and say a special prayer. In this way, every calamity was averted.

Years passed, and in the time of Nagid of Mezritch, disaster threatened again. He went into the forest and said, 'God, Lord of the Universe, I do not know how to light the sacred fire, but I remember the holy place in the forest, and I still know the special prayer.' He said the special prayer in the holy place and returned home to find that the calamity had been averted.

Many years later, when Rabbi Moshed-Leib of Sasov found trouble threatening his people, he went to the holy place in the forest and said, 'God, Lord of the Universe, I still know the holy place in the forest, but I do not know how to light the sacred fire and I have forgotten the special prayer. But O Lord, have pity on us and save your people.' Yet again, the tragedy was averted.

Finally, in the days of Rabbi Israel of Rizhyn, disaster threatened again. Sitting in his home, the Rabbi prayed to God from the depths of his heart. 'Sorry, Lord, I do not know the holy place in the forest, I cannot light the sacred fire, and worst of all, I have even forgotten the special prayer. Yet O God, have pity on us and deliver us from danger.' God listened to him and calamity was averted again.

A Hasidic story

QUESTIONS FOR DISCUSSION

1. Why did all the rabbis of the story obtain the same blessings from God, although they had progressively forgotten how to find the holy place, how to light the sacred fire, and how to recite the special prayer?

2. What is the meaning and value of holy places? Who made them holy? In what sense are they holy?

3. Can God be found outside holy places? Should we completely reject the idea of holy places? Why? What is their real value?

4. Do pilgrimages to holy places have any value? What is it? Why are people so fond of them? What purpose do pilgrimages fulfil?

5. What is the meaning of sacred rites like the holy fire of the story? Are they necessary to worship God? Are they convenient? How did they come to be? What is their value?

6. Should we do away with all sacred rites and rituals? Why?

7. What is the meaning of 'special prayers'? Who formulated them? How did they become special? What is their value? Do we need them?

8. Can we pray without prayers? How? Why? Should we do away with all special prayers? Why?

9. What is the internal connection between 'prayer' and 'prayers'?

POINTS FOR REFLECTION

1. The effectiveness of our prayer lies in our faith in God and our love for him and for others.

2. God knows our needs even before we ask him.

3. Jesus said to the Samaritan woman, God has to be worshipped in spirit and in truth, not in this place or that place.

5. Places of pilgrimage are good, but God is found everywhere. He dwells in the depths of everyone's heart.

6. With continued use, we 'sacralize' rites and rituals. We make the fire, the water and other elements sacred. Rites are external signs – good in themselves – of internal realities such as our faith and

our love and devotedness to God. They are means, not ends in themselves. They change according to circumstances of time, place and culture.

7. By frequent repetition, we 'absolutise' our prayers. We make special prayers out of the fortuitous but passing formulations of someone else's religious experience. Prayers do not have any power in themselves independently of the faith of the person who recites them.

The saviours

When human beings emerged on the face of the earth, the animals became alarmed. It would no longer be safe for them to live in the open air.

The moles were the most anxious of all. Their frightened leader addressed them:

'Friends, it is no longer safe for us to live on the surface of the earth. We shall not survive with so many threats to our health and well-being. The only solution is for us to withdraw. Let us burrow deep into the earth where we will be able to live protected from these corrupt and perilous surroundings.'

The moles drilled their tunnels far beneath the surface of the earth and began their hidden, subterranean existence. Cut off from the outside world, their lives were arduous, but they felt secure. To cope with their new environment, they had to develop different ways of living and working. They had to formulate a new philosophy of life and to adopt a new value system. There was very little air to breathe and food was scarce. In order to survive, it was essential to form a strong community. The moles were forbidden from having personal friendships, close relationships or an active social life. Their lives became highly disciplined and regimented. Their leaders kept up a steady stream of propaganda:

'Dear brother and sister moles, we are a lucky lot. We have been saved from the contamination and dangers of the world outside. We are a chosen species. Out there in the world, our brother and sister animals are being threatened and corrupted. We alone are living healthy, pure and fulfilled lives. God has saved us from the corruption of the world so that we may inspire others to follow our example.'

All the moles echoed these inspiring slogans.

'We have been saved from the corruption and dangers of the world.'

'We are a chosen species. We are an inspiration for others to follow.'

So enthusiastic were they that many moles rose up and said to their companions,

'If only those wretched animals in the world outside could witness the quality of our lives, the strength of our community, the happiness of our existence, they would readily follow our example and be saved. Come. Let us go out into that wicked world to preach our gospel of salvation to our brothers and sisters in order to bring them into our burrows.'

The moles went up to the surface, full of zeal and concern for their terrestrial brothers and sisters. As they emerged from the darkness into the sunlight, their eyes smarted with the intensity of the colours, their ears ached with the unfamiliar sounds, their lungs gasped in the blast of fresh air, and their thick black fur made it impossible for them to bear the heat of the sun. They retreated back into their burrows as fast as they could, and were never again seen on the surface of the earth.

QUESTIONS FOR DISCUSSION

1. How did the moles avoid the threats and dangers of the world? How did they save themselves?

2. Did they really improve themselves and the quality of their lives?

3. Why was it necessary for the leaders of the moles to keep indoctrinating and brainwashing their followers?

4. How do you think it was possible for the moles to believe themselves to be better than others and even to be models for others to follow?

5. What happened to them when they came out of their burrows to convert their fellow animals in the world outside?

6. Can you apply the story of the moles to modern religious groups, denominations, sects and organisations?

POINTS FOR REFLECTION

1. If we are to have anything relevant to say to people, we must be in touch with the reality of their lives.

2. True faith is open and trusting towards others. It does not need ideologies, highly organised communities and brainwashing techniques to spread its message.

The strawberry

A Zen master was being chased by a tiger. He ran and ran until he reached the edge of a precipice. There he climbed down into the branches of a tree growing out of a crevice to escape from the animal.

With horror, he realized that he was too heavy for the tree and the branches were beginning to break. Above him crouched the tiger, waiting to devour him. Below him was an abyss ready to swallow him. Death seemed inevitable. He was terrified.

He looked up and saw a wild strawberry bush growing on the cliff face, its fruit red and inviting. The master picked a strawberry and put it in his mouth. He closed his eyes and savoured its taste. 'Strawberry, how sweet you are,' he said in delight.

QUESTIONS FOR DISCUSSION

1. Do you think people are happy throughout their lives and throughout the moments of every day? Why?

2. Is it easy for us to enjoy the here-and-now, without regretting the past or worrying about the future? Why?

3. Is there a secret formula for finding happiness and peace of mind? What might it be?

4. Consider the story and ask yourself: Do I regret the missed opportunities of the past? Am I ridden with guilt and scruples over my past misdeeds? Am I tense and anxious about the future? Do I keep fearing the worst? Do I enjoy the small joys and pleasures of my daily life?

POINTS FOR REFLECTION

1. Life is given to us mortals moment by moment. The only moment that counts is the present. The here-and-now is all we have.

2. The past is gone and will never return. The future is not yet here and may never arrive.

3. If we cannot enjoy the present moment, we will never find joy in life. If we are dead to the here-and-now, then we are not alive but only surviving.

4. We spoil the beauty of the present by pining for the past and worrying about the future.

5. The present moment is the point of intersection between God's eternal life and our temporal lives.

The here-and-now is the sacrament of God's presence.

6. If we cannot find God in the present, we cannot find him at all.

7. We need to leave the past in the hands of an all-forgiving God, the future in the hands of an all-provident God, and to live the present in the hands of an all-loving God.

The watchman

There was once a castle surrounded by a vast desert. Occasionally a lonely caravan stopped there, but apart from that, life in the castle was monotonous, hardly changing from day to day and from year to year.

Then one day, the King sent a message: 'Be prepared. We have been told that God plans to visit our country, and he will stop at your castle. Be ready to receive him.'

The officials who lived in the castle followed the King's instructions. They arranged for the walls to be painted and the rooms to be cleaned, and they ordered the watchman to stay alert for any sign that God was approaching. The watchman was filled with pride. Never before had such an important task been entrusted to him.

He stood in his watchtower day and night, scanning the horizon, constantly alert and on the look-out for signs of God's presence. Often he wondered to himself, 'What will God look like? Will he arrive with a large retinue? Will he be accompanied by a powerful army?'

Absorbed in such thoughts, the faithful guard spent weeks and months watching and waiting, full of hope, while inside the castle, the officials and solders had forgotten all about God's visit.

After many years, the watchman felt himself growing weary. 'Will God never arrive?' he asked himself. 'Why is he taking so long to come? Will he even want to meet a poor man like me when he gets here?'

He went on scanning the empty skyline until his eyesight began to fail and he could hardly move or hear or see. He knew that his end was near. Sadly he murmured, 'I have spent my whole life waiting for God. All I ever wanted was to see him, but he did not come. Were all my hopes in vain?'

Then a voice spoke to him, and it was so close it seemed to come from inside his own heart. 'Don't you recognize me? Can't you see me? I am here beside you, within you.'

The watchman was bewildered but full of joy. 'My God,' he said. 'Is it really you? Have you come at last? What's wrong with me? I never heard you or saw you coming. But why did you make me wait so long?'

Sweetly, the voice replied: 'From the very moment you decided to wait for me, I have been within you. I have been here all along. Don't you know the secret? Only those who wait for me will see me.'

A wonderful sense of peace filled the watchman. 'So you were within me, and I was looking for you outside,' he said. 'How foolish I've been. Now I know the secret. I can go in peace.'

QUESTIONS FOR DISCUSSION

1. What meaning can you find in this story for our lives?

2. Can we really find God in this world? How?

3. What do the castle, the people living there, and the watchman represent?

4. Does God make us wait for a long time before he comes to us? Why?

5. Who are those to whom God shows himself first? Why?

6. What are the attitudes necessary to receive God?

7. If we apprehend God with our inner vision, how would you describe that vision?

POINTS FOR REFLECTION

1. To long for God is to experience his presence.

2. Think about the following New Testament characters and the ways in which their experiences reflect the lessons of the story: the three kings, the old man Simeon, Anna the prophetess, Mary the mother of Jesus, Peter, Nathanael, the good thief, the centurion at the foot of the cross. Can you think of others?

The wisest of them all

Gaspar, Melchior, Balthazar and Artaban mounted their camels and set off on a journey, their destination unknown, their guide a twinkling star that had appeared in the western sky, their goal – to pay homage to the newborn King of kings.

The magi had sold all they possessed to buy gifts worthy of a king. Gaspar, Melchior and Balthazar had bought gold, frankincense and myrrh. Artaban had chosen precious gems – a ruby, emeralds and diamonds.

As he journeyed along, Artaban gazed at the precious gems in the palm of his hand and said to himself, 'How I long for the day when I will meet my King and offer him these gifts. That will be the greatest day of my life.'

His daydream was interrupted by pitiful groans and moans. Somebody was in pain! Quickly, he put the gems away in his purse, dismounted and went in search of whoever was suffering. He found the man in a ditch, half-naked, bleeding and battered. He had been attacked by robbers and left there to die.

Artaban's heart went out to the man. He lifted him gently onto his camel and took him to a nearby inn. He

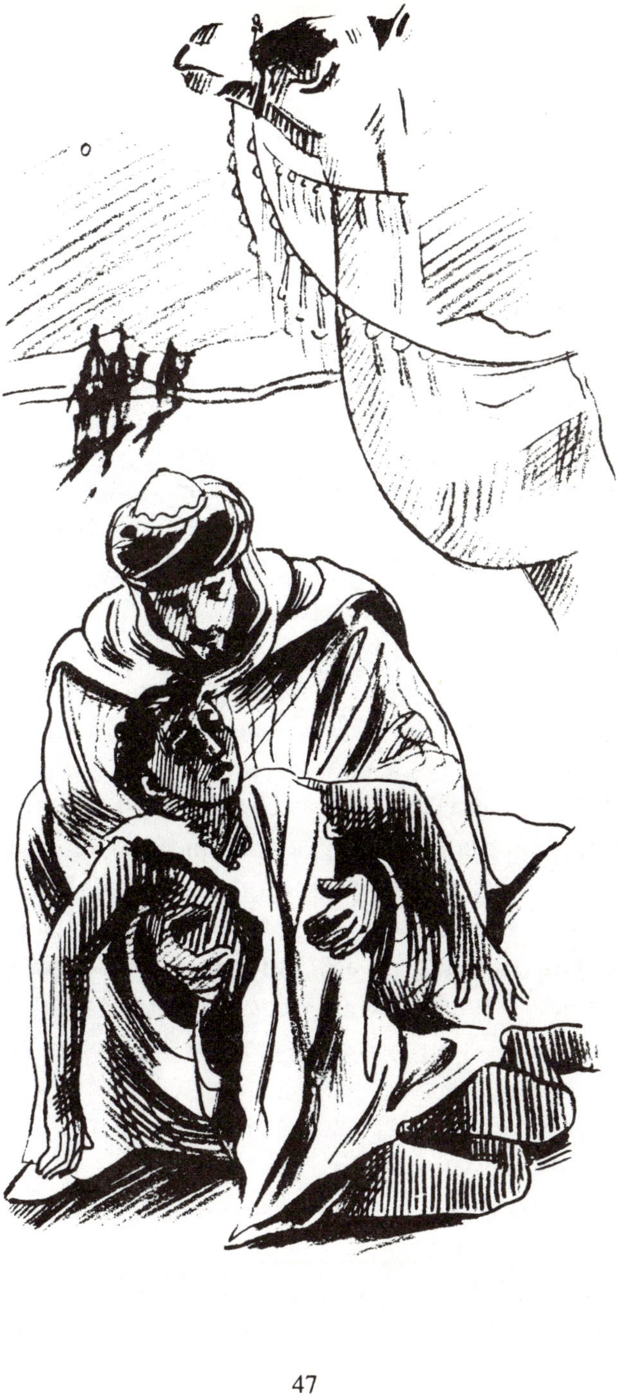

cared for him with such devotion that he forgot about the star, the journey ahead and the newborn King. When he was sure that the man was recovering and would be taken care of, he prepared to set out on his travels again. The innkeeper stopped him at the door and demanded payment for the man's keep. All Artaban had were the precious stones. Without hesitation, he dipped into his purse for the ruby and gave it to the innkeeper. He hurried away to look for his travelling companions, telling himself,

'Never mind the ruby. My King will not take it amiss that I gave it away to save a man's life.'

He searched and searched, but he had lost the trail of the other magi and the star had vanished from the sky. At last, limp with exhaustion, Artaban sat down on a tree stump and prayed:

'My King of kings, I left my home, my family and my country to find you. Now I am lost and alone in a trackless wilderness. Guide my steps, Lord, so that I may find you and offer you my precious gifts.'

Rising, he remounted his camel and set out again. Day after weary day he journeyed on without friends for company or a star to guide him, past bustling towns and sleepy hamlets and palm-fringed oases, determined to find his King. Deep in his heart he knew that some day, somewhere, somehow, he would find him.

Once, tired and thirsty, he sat down to rest by a well. In the distance he saw a caravan trailing towards him. Maybe the travellers would have news of his King! But when they came closer he saw that it was a convoy of death, slave traders dragging their human cargo across the desert. They would have no news for him.

They too stopped at the oasis to rest, and Artaban looked at the emaciated, frightened slaves with great compassion and love, knowing that they were condemned to lifelong bondage. Seeing his pity and gentleness, the slaves flocked around him with heart-rending cries: 'Please sir, buy us all, buy us all and free us from the hands of these brutal men. If you buy us, we will serve you for the rest of our lives!' Artaban's heart melted. He took the emeralds and the diamonds out of his purse. It was a royal price to pay for freedom. As if compelled by a force beyond himself, he stood up and approached the caravaneers. 'I buy them, all of them,' he said.

Astonished, the slave traders asked, 'What have you to offer us in exchange?'

Artaban opened his hand and the jewels glistened in the desert sun. 'This is the price,' he said. 'It is a bounty worthy of a king.'

The traders took the ransom and said, 'The slaves are yours, all of them.'

Artaban turned to the slaves and told them joyfully, 'You are free! You belong to yourselves now, not to me. Go home and live in peace.'

When they had all gone, Artaban was left alone and confused by the well. 'Have I done the right thing?' he asked himself. 'My heart tells me I'm right, but I have nothing left for my King.'

The sun set and darkness covered the desert. Artaban lifted his tear-stained face and gazed at the starry sky arching above him. Then in astonishment he exclaimed,

'It's there! Can it be true? Surely that is the star of the newborn King! I must follow it. But no, it's too late. I have nothing left to offer him. It's too late, too late for me to meet my King.'

He bowed his head and sobbed broken-heartedly. Then a mysterious voice spoke to him out of the darkness.

'It's not too late, Artaban. You came at the right time. I want you to know that yours were the first gifts I received after my birth. Of the four magi who set out in search of me, you were the first to find me, the first to pay homage to me, and the first to offer me his gifts.'

*Adapted from the story 'The Fourth Wise Man'
by Henry Van Dyke*

QUESTIONS FOR DISCUSSION

1. Did Artaban succeed in meeting Christ? Where?

2. Why should Artaban be called the wisest of them all?

3. What do the precious gems in the story symbolise?

4. Can you remember some stories in the Gospels which convey the same message as the story of Artaban? Explain what they mean.

5. In what ways does Jesus want us to serve him?

POINTS FOR REFLECTION

1. Jesus said that whatever we do to the least of his people, we do to him.

2. To respond in love to those in need is to offer God our most precious gifts.

PART 2

Parables on sociable and just values

A divided world

Long, long ago a group of adventurers built a boat and sailed towards the distant horizon. For months on end they ploughed through perilous seas, believing that one day, they would discover land.

At last, they sighted a small island rising out of the emptiness of the ocean. As they approached, they discovered that the island was unspoiled and beautiful beyond compare. They decided that they would make it their home.

They built a little cottage and began their new life. The water was pure and the air was clean. The soil was fertile and yielded an abundance of fruits. They were very happy in their new home.

One day, a cruise liner approached the island and the tourists on board spotted the cottage. 'Look,' said one of the tourists, 'There's a little house over there. The island must be inhabited. Let's stop and visit the people who live there.'

The tourists went ashore, and some of them were so enchanted with the island that they decided to return and settle there. Soon, news of the island's fertile beauty spread far and wide, and many people came to settle on that small paradise.

The islanders became increasingly alarmed by the crowds. 'At this rate, there will be no space left for us,' said one. 'We must be wise before it's too late.'

The wise islander and his friends began working through the night, furtively and in a great hurry, erecting fences around the most fertile parts of the land. They fixed signs and notices to the fences, the likes of which had never been seen on the island before: NO ENTRY, PRIVATE PROPERTY, TRESSPASSERS WILL BE PROSECUTED. Locks and iron gates began appearing among the fences.

Soon, the richest and most fertile part of the island was completely surrounded with barbed wire. The minority of the people, those who considered themselves 'wise', took possession of it all. By contrast, the majority, those who were not considered 'wise', found themselves pushed further and further towards the barren outskirts and rocky ledges, where they became destitute and homeless.

The wise minority built themselves palatial mansions and lived in the lap of luxury. When the poor looked through the gaps in the fences they saw food and clothing being thrown into dustbins and onto rubbish tips. In desperation, they called to those inside: 'Please, give us some of your food. We are starving out here.' 'If you want food, you will have to work for us,' replied the insiders.

The people on the outside, hungry and powerless, had no alternative but to work for those on the inside. In exchange, the insiders threw morsels of food over the fences, so meagre that they were barely enough to survive on.

The patience of the poor was slowly eroded, and

eventually they tried to pull the fences down with their bare hands. But the fences were strong and they did not succeed. They decided to organise themselves and to work together in order to break down the fences.

When the wise realized what was happening, they summoned the stronger and more influential, those who were becoming leaders among the poor, and coaxed them inside with words such as these:

'Please join us inside our fences. You will have as much food as you can eat, and we will give you many luxuries and privileges. In return, you will defend our fences and protect us against the onslaught of outsiders. You will become our army, our police and our security guards.'

Many of the poor joined the ranks of the insiders, and so THE ARMY was born.

Then the leaders of the wise turned their attention to the more intellectual and clever among the poor, and cajoled them too:

'If you join us, we will give you all the facilities you need to study and do research. We shall build you schools and colleges and teach you all we know. In return, you must teach those outside to listen to us, to live in peace and to respect the established law and order of the island.'

So many more of the poor joined the insiders. They became the philosophers and thinkers, the intelligentsia of the society inside the fence. In this way, CAPITALIST IDEOLOGY AND CULTURE were born.

Next, the leaders of the 'wise' addressed the most pious, religious-minded and devout of the poor and seduced them thus:

'Come and join us, and we will build you beautiful

seminaries and churches, and impressive theological colleges. You will be able to spend time in prayer and reflection, and in return you must preach to the outsiders meekness, forgiveness, resignation to the will of God and obedience to those in authority.'

Many of the outsiders agreed, and in this way they were deluded into joining the ranks of the insiders. They became religious leaders, preachers, interpreters of God's will. And so, RELIGIOUS IDEOLOGIES AND STRUCTURES were born.

By these means, systems of oppression and exploitation were perpetrated for long, long years, until at last some of the insiders became aware that they had been unjust to their weaker brothers and sisters outside the fences.

Some of the strong realized that if the weak united and worked together, they could overcome their defences and weapons and bring down the fences.

Some of the intelligentsia discovered that outside the fences existed values which could not be found in their universities and academic books, values such as solidarity, unity, co-operation and sharing.

Some of the religious-minded people remembered that Christ, the Son of God, was born, lived and died outside the fence.

The insiders who had realized all these things tried to move outside the fences, to work for and with the poor. But they faced enormous opposition. The great majority of those on the inside considered them renegades and troublemakers. Many of those on the outside were indifferent to their well-meaning efforts. There was prejudice on every side.

In spite of all the efforts of those enlightened

insiders, things continued as they were. People outside the fences kept dying through hunger, exploitation and neglect.

But why should we continue with this story? Do we lack the courage to recognise that the world we live in is an island, a vast island, thickly populated, beautiful and fertile? Dare we acknowledge that it is also a lonely island, an island divided by a fence separating the rich from the poor, the 'haves' from the 'have-nots', the wealthy nations from the under-developed ones?

I ask myself for how much longer things must go on like this in our little world. Is there no remedy? Can we not heal the divide which mars our beautiful planet, our EARTH?

An adaptation from a Spanish audiovisual

QUESTIONS FOR DISCUSSION

1. Is the story of a divided world just make-believe, or does it really exist?

2. What is the barbed wire? What does it stand for, and what do the notices attached to it signify?

3. Are barbed wire fences sometimes justified? When? Who for?

4. Who do those inside the fences represent?

5. Who are those outside the fences?

6. Who are those from the outside – the strong, the clever, the pious – who agree to join the insiders? How did their institutions come into existence?

7. Who are the exploiters and exploited in our world?

8. Who are those insiders who work to help those on the outside?

POINTS FOR REFLECTION

1. The island represents our world, our country, our city, our schools and parishes and even our homes. It is human society.

2. Fences are erected by attitudes of greed, violence, selfishness, manipulation and the longing for power. It is the desire to possess exclusively for oneself which leads to war and conflict.

3. The parable does not pass moral judgement on individuals but describes a social reality. The army, the intelligentsia, organised religion, are all part of a social structure which is in itself oppressive and unjust. In most cases, those who benefit from our unjust social structures act in good faith.

4. In our unjust world, we are all both exploiters and exploited.

5. We cannot close our eyes and submit to an unjust social order, especially if we are its beneficiaries.

Many of our cultural and religious values and institutions are socially and economically manipulated, not just in the interests of money but in the interests of serving those with power and influence in society.

6. Social reformers and activists have to face misunderstanding, criticism and persecution from their own brothers and sisters, and indifference and lack ofinterest from outsiders.

7. Many outsiders have formed such a poor self-image and have become so fatalistic towards their suffering that it is hard to stir them into action.

Dream or reality?

Countless ages ago, among all the galaxies and stars of the universe, there was a small planet. The planet was inhabited by two intelligent and loving races called the 'Daylings' and the 'Nightlings'. Their differences complemented one another, and they lived in harmony and peace.

The daylings were conscious and active only during the hours of daylight. As the sun dipped beneath the horizon, they fell into a deep and dreamless sleep from which nothing could rouse them until the dawn.

As soon as the first light of morning touched their eyelids, the daylings awoke and resumed their activities, without ever being aware of the long hours of darkness. They were under the illusion that life consisted of unending sunlit days.

By contrast, the nightlings became active only when the sun disappeared and darkness covered the planet. Just before sunrise they fell asleep, and there they stayed, oblivious to everything, until the last light of the day had vanished. They believed that the darkness of night was the only reality. They knew nothing of the daylight hours which passed while they were asleep.

The daylings and the nightlings were creative and

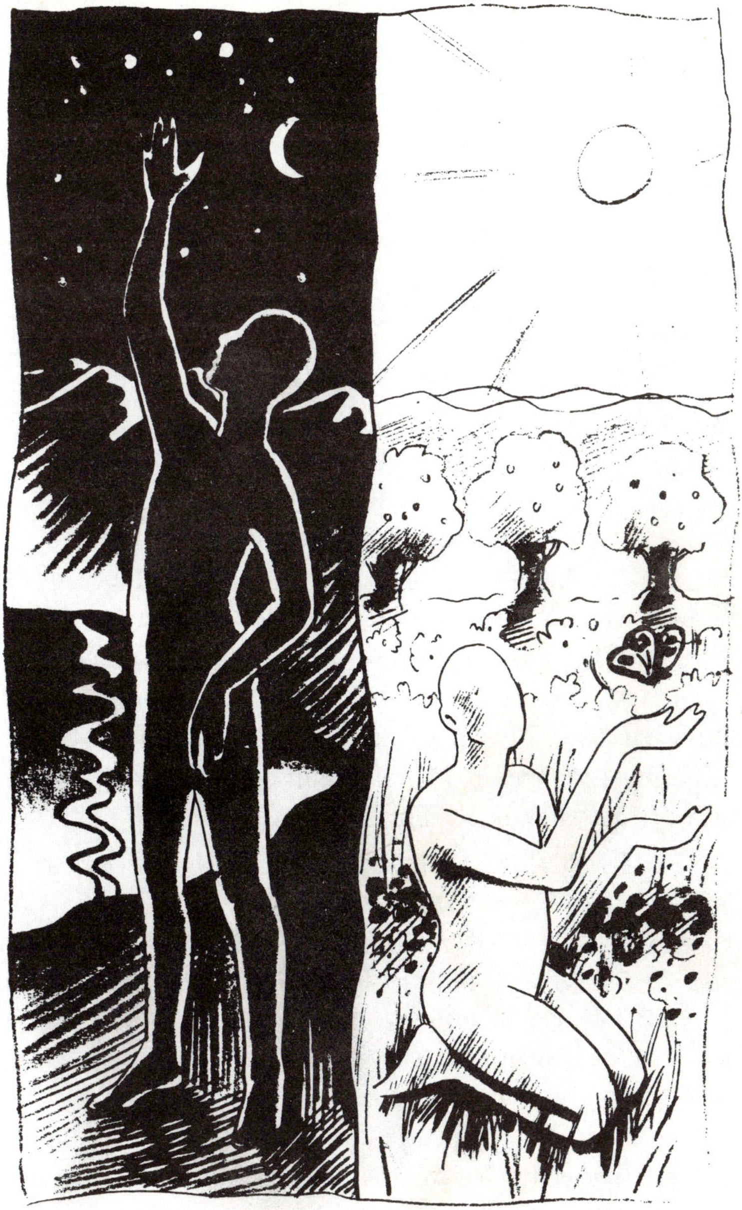

clever. Over the years, they explored the world in which they lived and grew to appreciate its many wonders.

The nightlings were enthralled by the majesty of the heavens. They became great astronomers and wrote learned treatises on the patterns and movements of the night sky. They loved the pale beauty of a moonlit landscape, the chiaroscuro of light and shade on the mountain tops. They wrote sublime poetry in praise of the shimmer of starlight on water and the dark mysteries of the forest.

The daylings celebrated the brightness and warmth of their world. They wrote scholarly books on heat and light. In words and pictures they depicted the delicate hues of a butterfly's wings, the colourful beauty of wildflowers, the many shades of green in the forest canopy. They sang of blue skies and sunlit gardens.

At last, there came a time when the daylings discovered the scientific and literary works of the nightlings. As they read them, their curiosity gradually gave way to bewilderment and confusion.

'What's all this?' they asked each other. 'Constellations? Stars? A full moon? Silvery streams?'

They searched and searched, but they could not discover the whereabouts of the stars or the galaxies. They could find no mountains bathed in moonlight, or quiet lakes beneath a dark sky.

Eventually, frustrated and bemused, they said to one another, 'These people are dream merchants and storytellers. They know nothing of reality. They can tell us nothing about our world.'

The nightlings too discovered the writings of the daylings. In vain, they tried to find blue skies and sunshine. They hunted for hedgerows speckled with brightly-coloured flowers, and peered into the treetops trying to glimpse the iridescent flash of a kingfisher's wings. 'These works are nonsense,' they said, when all their efforts had failed. 'The people who wrote these books must be either liars or fools. They have no knowledge, no understanding of the real world.'

The daylings and the nightlings no longer explored the mysteries of nature. They no longer wrote poetry and studied their environment. Instead, they spent all their time writing lengthy critiques on each other's work, challenging and refuting the other's perceptions and evaluations.

They grew suspicious of one another, and their criticisms became increasingly hostile and abusive. Enmity sprang up between them, until at last they said to themselves,

'These people are dangerous. They undermine our established beliefs and traditions. If we let them, they will subvert our value system and destroy our culture. They are a threat to civilized society.'

War broke out between the daylings and the nightlings. It was a strange war, silent and cold-blooded, more deadly even than wars fought with bombs and guns and swords. At night, the nightlings murdered the sleeping daylings, and during the day the daylings killed the defenceless nightlings.

So it was that life was destroyed in their world. The planet continued to whirl, silent and deserted, among the spheres, with nobody left to hymn the bright marvels of the day and the moonlit mysteries of the night.

QUESTIONS FOR DISCUSSION

1. Who do the daylings and the nightlings represent?

2. Why did they see things differently?

3. Were they mistaken or dishonest when they wrote their beautiful poems and scientific works?

4. Why were they unable to accept one another's ideas?

5. What was the consequence of their inability to understand each other?

6. Why are there so many conflicts and wars in our world – between individuals, among families, between nations and religious groups?

7. Are different views of reality – man, the world and God – necessarily contradictory? Why?

8. What do we mean by saying that our society is 'pluralistic'? Can there be peace in such a society? How?

9. Can we hold absolute and unchangeable views about man, the world and God? Why?

POINTS FOR REFLECTION

1. Our ideas about reality are conditioned by the society into which we are born, our cultural and reli-

gious milieu, the time and the place in which we live.

2. The daylings and the nightlings were both completely correct in what they said and wrote, yet they had experienced only half of what there was to experience.

3. Seemingly opposite statements are not necessarily contradictory. For example, the statements 'God is all justice' and 'God is all forgiveness' can both be true. What would be contradictory would be to say, 'God is only justice' and 'God is only forgiveness'.

4. People of different religious traditions have different but not necessarily contradictory ideas of God. Each one is trying to express in an imperfect, human way what he or she has experienced of and thinks about God. All statements about God are partial, even if they are true – we cannot comprehend God's fullness.

5. It is part of our nature to conceptualise our perceptions, to make judgements and build systems of philosophy and theology. These may all be different, while still having their own coherence and logic within the premises and experiences of our particular environments.

6. When people indulge in heated controversies and have acrimonious arguments about their beliefs, it often has more to do with blindness and ignorance than with deliberate ill-will.

7. When we deny the insights, visions and perceptions of others, we deny ourselves the means to grow in our understanding and our knowledge. Through dialogue and mutual understanding, people of different religious traditions can come to a more comprehensive knowledge of God, while bearing in mind that God is ultimately a mystery, beyond all our human concepts.

8. We can love and celebrate our own beliefs and traditions while still respecting the value of other beliefs and traditions. Being different does not mean being unequal in knowledge, integrity or truth.

Greedy Timothy

Timothy was a greedy man. He never had enough money and possessions. He was constantly fighting with his neighbours over money matters.

One day one of his enemies decided to destroy Timothy. Very cunningly, he presented him with a small 'goldfish' in a glass bowl. He told him, 'Timothy, when this goldfish grows to its full size and dies a natural death, its body will turn into pure gold. You will be rich beyond your wildest dreams.'

Timothy's insatiable greed got the better of his common sense and he believed the story of the goldfish. He was beside himself with joy and very grateful to his enemy.

He took the fish home and kept it in a small tank. He fed it generously, and to his delight it grew and grew until it was too big for the tank. At great expense he had a pond built for the fish, and then a small lake. All the time, he was dreaming of the day when he would get his gold.

After many years, Timothy had used all his savings and spent all his days feeding and caring for the fish, which still kept growing. He longed for it to die so that

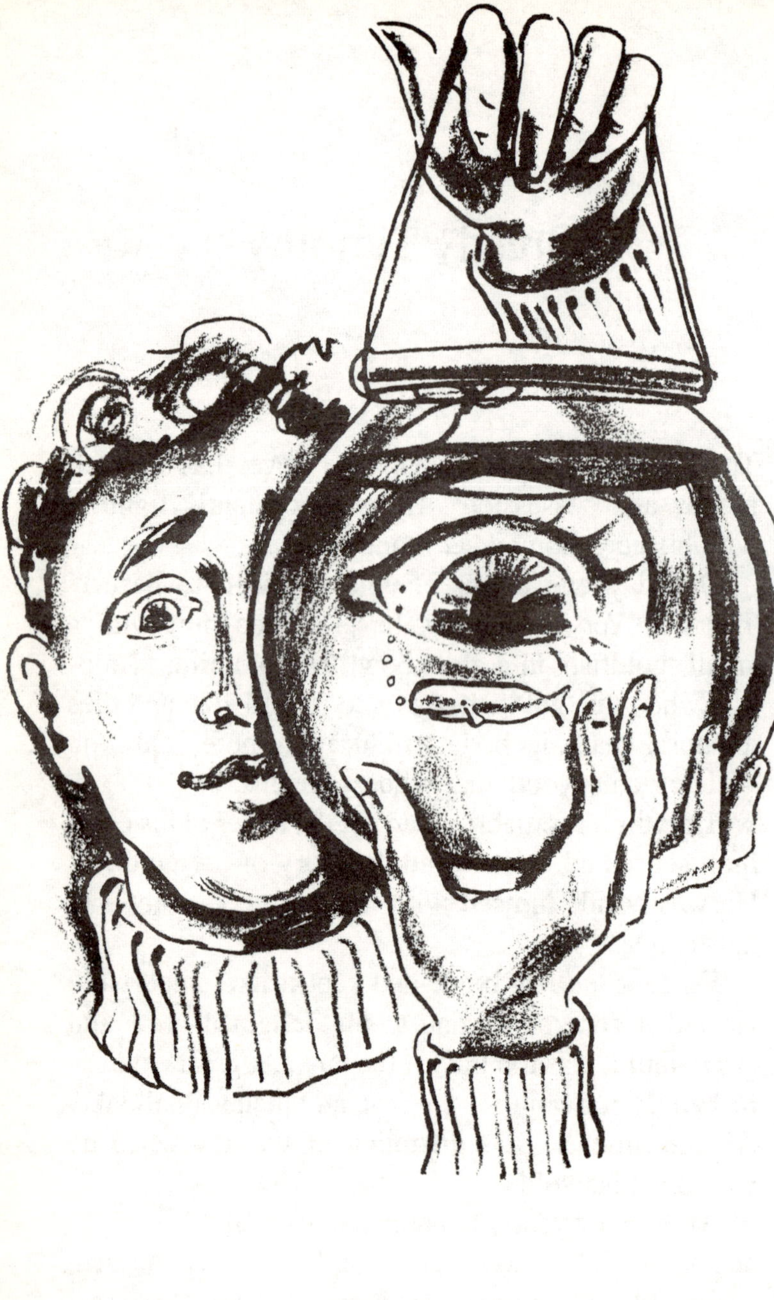

he would become rich. Eventually, bankrupt and old, Timothy died before the fish.

He never found out that his enemy had presented him with a whale.

QUESTIONS FOR DISCUSSION

1. Is money a blessing or a curse? Why?

2. Is money dangerous? What are the dangers of money?

3. Can a greedy person be happy? How?

4. Is it money or greed that is the root of all evil?

5. Is money *necessary* to live a happy life?

6. Is money *sufficient* to live a happy life?

7. Why does Jesus say that it is hard for a rich man to enter the Kingdom of Heaven?

8. Is the teaching of Scripture opposed to money? In what way?

9. Is it true to say that money is the idol of modern man?

10. As a rule, do you think people are greedy for money? What are the consequences of this?

POINTS FOR REFLECTION

1. Most of us are like Timothy. We sacrifice the best we have (time, energy, love and friendship) in the pursuit of wealth which we never achieve.

2. Happiness lies not in having what we want, but in wanting what we have.

Please, help me!

A fish was washed onto the beach by a violent wave. However hard he struggled, he could not get back into the water. Desperately, he kept calling for help: 'Please, help me! I am gasping for breath. Please, somebody put me back in the sea.'

A rich man passed by and heard the cries of the fish. 'I wish I could help you,' he said, 'but I'm on my way to the bank and I'm already late. I'm so sorry. Please, excuse me.'

The fish kept struggling and calling out, until he attracted the attention of a passing tourist. 'I'd like to help you,' said the tourist, 'but I don't know what to do. If only I had something I could use to push you back into the sea, but I've brought nothing with me. I'm on holiday, you see.'

'Use a stick or a twig, or just pick me up in your hand. Please, please put me back in the sea,' said the fish.

The tourist looked doubtful. 'I suppose I could do that, but on second thoughts, it's probably better if you help yourself. I'm sure you'll find a way to save yourself if you try. After all, "where there's a will there's a way".' He took a photograph of the dying fish and went away.

A woman walked past and heard the cries of the fish. He begged her to help him: 'I'm dying. Please, put me back in the sea. Please, hurry. I can't survive much longer.'

The woman looked sympathetic, but she said, 'Before I can help you, I need to know your case history. Tell me everything that happened to put you in this situation.'

The fish told her everything about himself, his family, his past life, his interests and beliefs. The woman listened carefully, then she said, 'Before I put you back in the sea, I want you to reflect carefully upon how you came to be here in the first place. You must make sure that once I return you to the sea, you never get yourself into this kind of situation again.'

By that time, the fish had died. The woman shook her head regretfully and went away.

An old man passed by and looked at the dead fish. 'How cruel the sea is,' he said dispassionately. 'No point in worrying about the fish, for what can be done? That's life. It's nobody's fault.'

The beach remained silent and deserted for a long time. The tide crept in and a friendly wave lifted the body of the fish and returned it to the sea. The tourist, passing by again, saw the fish in the water and said, 'You see! I was right! If a person really wants to help himself, there's always a way. That fish has gone back into the sea.'

An adaptation from the script of
a Spanish audiovisual

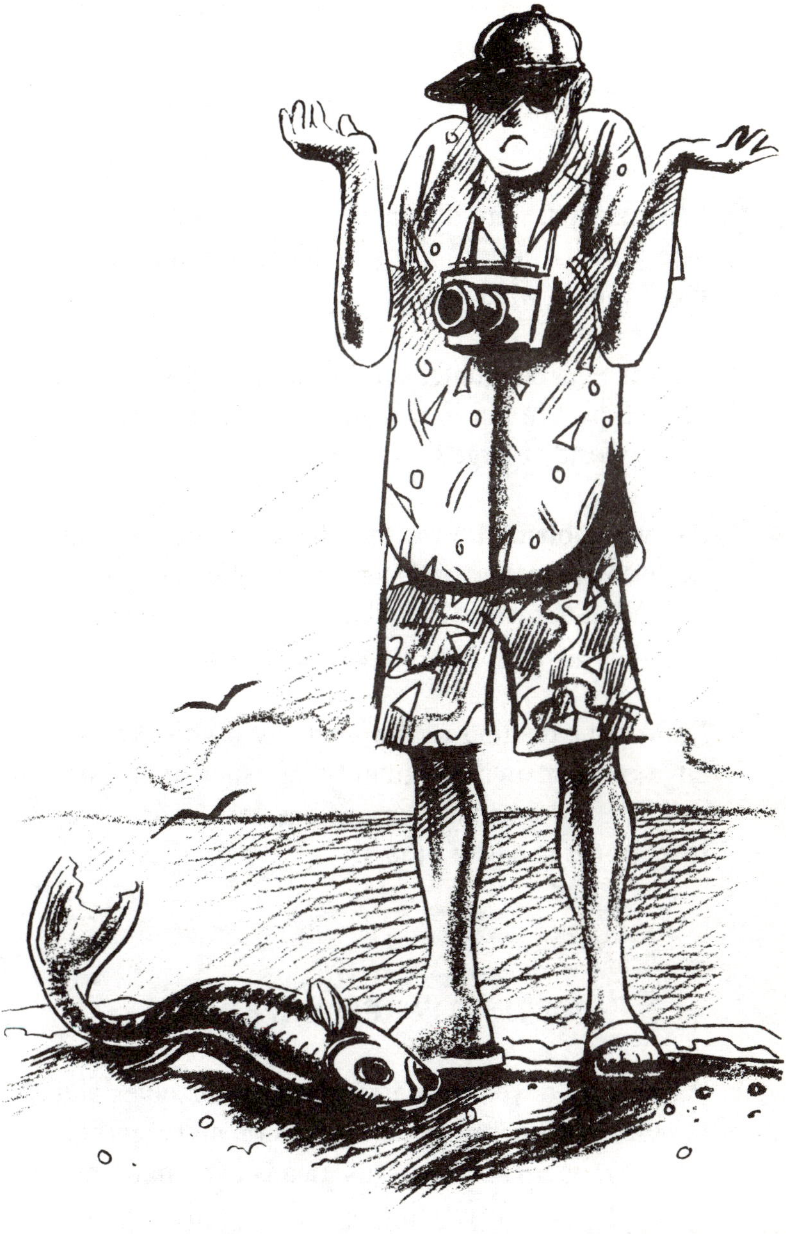

QUESTIONS FOR DISCUSSION

1. Does the story reflect the realities of our lives? How?

2. What attitudes are displayed by the different characters in the story? Do you identify with any of them, and in what way?

3. Do you ever encounter such attitudes in your home, school, parish, place of work, society, country, and in the world at large?

4. Are we to blame for the fact that there are so many destitute, homeless and starving people in our society and in our world? In what ways are we to blame or not to blame? If we are not to blame, who is?

5. From your reading of the media and your knowledge of your own community and society, discuss examples of non-interference and lack of involvement in the needs of others.

POINTS FOR REFLECTION

1. We need to develop an awareness in ourselves and in others of the injustices, oppression and exploitation of modern society. This means examining our consciences and questioning the reasons we give for doing nothing.

2. When a Master of the Law asked Jesus, 'Who is my neighbour?', Jesus replied by telling the parable of the Good Samaritan. We are called to show ourselves to be neighbour to those in need. It is not in our physical proximity or our shared interests and values that we become good neighbours, but in our response to the cries of those in need.

The swallow and the frogs

Hidden in the woods among tangled undergrowth, there was an abandoned well. The sun never managed to penetrate the overhanging trees, so the well was gloomy and dank and inhabited only by frogs.

Swallows nested in the trees, flying happily from branch to branch and enjoying the warmth of the sunshine and the brightly-coloured flowers. But the frogs in the well were a bit like humans. They were always busy, working hard day after day in a world without colour or fragrance, without variety or beauty, without freedom. Their only aim in life was to produce more and more, and they worked under the constant vigilance of their bosses, the big frogs. The big frogs were wealthy and powerful. The small frogs were poor, depressed and apathetic.

One summer day when a trickle of sunlight had crept into the well, a daring swallow flew down to see what was in there. Swooping in and out of the gloom, she sang of joy and freedom. Her song invited the frogs to find a better way of living, to experience sunny days and blue skies, to discover the pleasures of love and friendship.

The little frogs listened in amazement, but

suddenly the big frogs interrupted the swallow's song: 'What are you doing, you stupid frogs, listening to all this nonsense about freedom and love? What matters is increased productivity and higher profits. Don't take any notice of that crazy bird, coming in here to disrupt the peace and threaten our prosperity. Get back to work. In the real world there are more important things than love and friendship.'

That night, the frogs found it impossible to sleep. They lay awake, thinking about the swallow's words, wondering if what she said was true. The next day, they held a secret meeting among themselves.

'The swallow was right,' they said. 'There must be more to life than work. We want to enjoy a better life, with time to relax and enjoy one another's company. We don't want to work for the big frogs any more. We want to be in control of our own lives.'

Soon after that, there was a revolution in the well. The small frogs resisted the big frogs, and after a long and painful struggle they defeated their exploiters. At last they were free. They had leisure time, and they could afford luxuries and comforts to make their lives easier. They were very happy in the bottom of their well, and they were grateful to the swallow who have given them the courage and inspiration to change their lives.

But gradually, they began to find life boring and unsatisfying. In their hearts, they became aware of a sense of futility, of a longing for something more than material prosperity and comfort. What's wrong with us?' they asked themselves. Why have we so quickly lost the happiness and peace of mind which the swallow promised us? We were hoping for something better than this. This is not what we wanted.'

One day, the little swallow appeared again, fluttering into the murky darkness of the well. 'What are you doing down here, living in this prison with your money and your luxuries? How can you endure such narrow, self-centred lives? Come! Leave the security of your well, come up into the light, make new friends and discover the needs of others. Share what you have with them. Only then will you find the fuller life I promised you when I first came into your well. You will find a world full of colour and fragrance, a world of love and friendship.'

The little frogs were very frightened. They felt so secure and protected in their well. But summoning all their courage, they decided to trust the swallow and follow her advice.

Outside the well, they found all that she had promised them. How liberating it was to shed their fear, to be free to love and to give. Only then did they understand the full meaning of the message the swallow had given them the first time she had flown into their well.

*An adaptation of the script of
a Spanish audiovisual*

QUESTIONS FOR DISCUSSION

1. Can you find parallels between this story and modern life?

2. What does the well represent?

3. Who do the big frogs stand for?

4. Who do the small frogs stand for?

5. What social values prevailed in the well?
6. Do you think there was exploitation in the well?

7. Who are the swallows in the real world, and do they have any way of communicating with the frogs? Do the small frogs listen to them?

POINTS FOR REFLECTION

1. Possessions and money alone cannot make us fully alive.

2. Unless we are willing to take risks and leave our old securities, we will never know true fulfilment.

3. It is in the interests of the rich and the powerful to stifle the voice of freedom and love.

Swimmy

There was a school of little fishes which lived happily in the ocean. One among them had such extraordinary qualities that her friends gave her a name. They called her 'Swimmy'.

One day a big fish swam alongside the school, looking for all the world like an innocent passerby until – snap – he turned round and swallowed them all. All except Swimmy, who managed to escape.

Swimmy escaped because, being small, she was very cautious whenever she saw a fish that was bigger than her. She was so quick and agile that she used to infuriate the big fish, swimming up to them and then darting away before they could catch her.

Swimmy was determined to explore all the beauties of her underwater world, and she would not let fear prevent her. When the rest of her friends were eaten, she bravely continued her voyages of discovery alone.

After a long time, she came across another school of little fishes just like herself. How happy she was to find company again! They listened, enthralled, as she described the sights she had seen and the places she had visited. She told them of the sad fate of the last school she had been part of, and they admitted that they too were very afraid of the big fish.

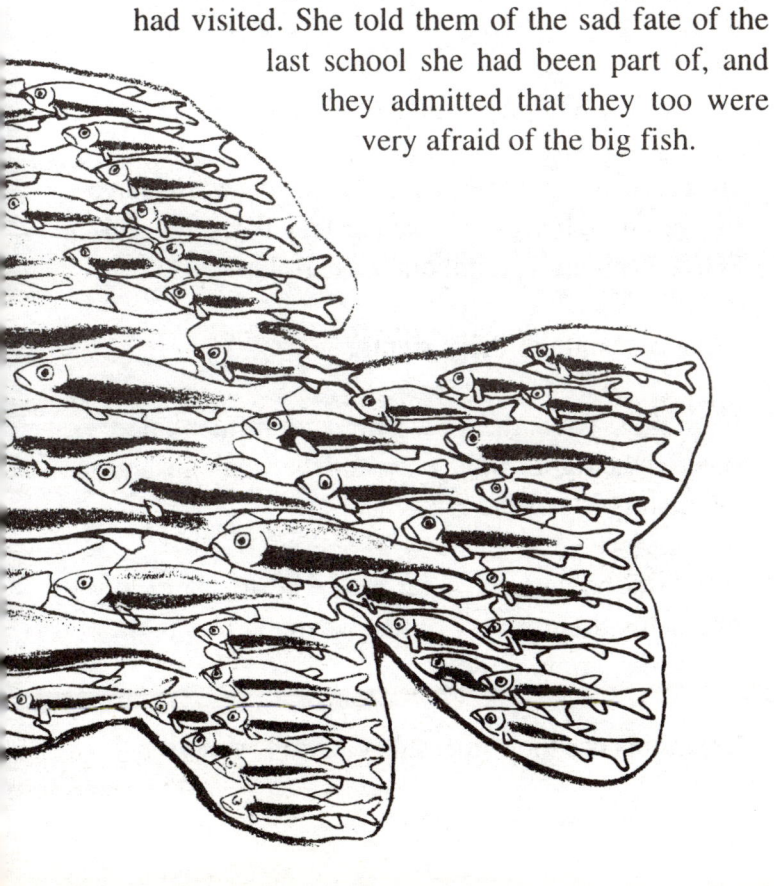

But Swimmy was wise and she had learned a great deal about survival on her lonely journeys across the ocean.

'Listen to me,' she said to the small fishes. 'There is only one way to stay alive and enjoy all that life has to offer. We must unite and stay together. Let's group ourselves in such a way that we look like an enormous fish, and that way we will frighten all the big fish and they will leave us alone.'

The little fishes clustered together in the shape of a fish, with Swimmy in the front as the watchful eye of the make-believe creature. Swimming together in formation, they explored the sea happy and undisturbed. From then on, the big fish feared and respected them.

QUESTIONS FOR DISCUSSION

1. Do the weak and the powerless of the world have the same rights as the strong and the powerful? Why? Who has given them those rights?

2. What are some of those rights?

3. In reality, have the powerful and influential respected the rights of the poor and the weak throughout history? Why?

4. Have the powerless so far managed to claim any rights for themselves? What weapons might they use if they are to do so?

5. Exploiters use the word 'subversive' to describe the

efforts of the exploited to claim their rights. Do you agree with this description? What is actually being subverted?

POINTS FOR REFLECTION

1. We all belong to groups and are members of society. It is for us to decide whether we group ourselves alongside the powerful or the powerless.

2. 'It is in the shelter of each other that the people live.' This traditional Irish saying reminds us that we are all responsible for one another and for the social structures which we belong to.

Teachers wanted

The animals who lived in the forest decided that the time had come to open a school for their little ones. The management in charge of the proposed school put an advertisement in the local papers which read as follows:

TEACHERS WANTED FOR NEW SCHOOL.
INTERVIEWS ON MONDAY MORNING. ONLY
THOSE WITH SUITABLE
QUALIFICATIONS NEED APPLY.

On Monday morning, prospective teachers lined up outside the interview room. First to appear before the selection committee was a sparrow. Timidly, she said,

'I should like to apply for the post of singing teacher.'

The committee began to question the little sparrow.

'Can you sing?' they asked. 'Are you an experienced singer?'

'Oh yes, I sing beautifully. I have been singing since the day I was born,' replied the sparrow. With that, she began to sing a tuneful and delicate melody. Abruptly, the management interrupted her.

'We're not interested in how well you can sing.

What we want to know is where you were trained, and what certificates and diplomas you have. We cannot consider your application unless you have suitable qualifications.'

The sparrow was taken aback.

'I can sing, as you heard, but I have no diplomas and certificates,' she said.

'In that case, we cannot employ you,' said the management brusquely. 'We are not interested in unqualified teachers.'

The next candidate to be interviewed was a dolphin.

'I'd like to be employed as a swimming coach in your new school,' he said.

'Where did you learn to swim?' asked the committee. 'Presumably you have some degree or certificate from a swimming institution?'

The dolphin shook his head regretfully.

'I'm sorry,' he said. 'I am an excellent swimmer and a kind and gentle teacher, but I have no qualifications.'

The committee dismissed him without listening any further.

'We are not willing to consider applications from those without qualifications,' they said.

One by one, the rest of the applicants came to be interviewed. The bees said,

'We would like to apply for jobs in the craft department of your school. Our hives are a marvel of intricate shapes and fine workmanship. We are patient and hardworking. We would be good craft teachers.' But on hearing that they had no certificates, the committee sent them away.

A deer applied to teach running lessons, and a monkey applied for a job as a gymnastics coach. A spider wanted to teach the children how to spin. All of them were turned down because they lacked the necessary qualifications.

In the end, the management committee decided that it was not possible to open a new school, because of the shortage of well-trained and qualified staff.

QUESTIONS FOR DISCUSSION

1. What lessons can we learn from this story?

2. What is happening in our schools and learning institutions?

3. Are degrees and certificates important? To what extent do they matter?

4. Should employment always be linked to degrees and high marks in examinations?

5. What sort of knowledge do colleges and universities impart?

6. What are the most important qualities in professions such as teaching?

POINTS FOR REFLECTION

1. Jesus Christ has probably been the subject of more academic studies and books than any other figure in history, yet he had no qualifications and left us no writings.

2. Education is a process which involves the whole human being. It goes far beyond the training which can be offered in institutions of learning.

3. A very exclusive 'education' may be a very poor education for life.

Things money cannot buy

Johnny was an ordinary man. He had little wealth but lots of happiness. He was contented and satisfied with his life.

One day as he was walking along the road, he found five hundred pounds in a dustbin. In surprise and disbelief, he picked up the bundle of notes. His first impulse was to take the money home, but on second thoughts he looked at the money in his hands and spoke to it thus:

'What treasure you are, but do I really need you? Until today, I never had you and I have been perfectly happy, while I have seen many of my neighbours who are loaded with notes like you, and yet they are miserable. I do not want to be like them. I would rather be what I am without you, than be what they are with you. No. I have no use of you.' And without further ado, he threw the notes back into the dustbin.

The notes were highly offended. They had never before been treated in such a shabby way. They shouted angrily at Johnny:

'Who do you think you are? You must be a complete idiot! Everybody else craves us and will do anything to possess us. How dare you treat us in this way?

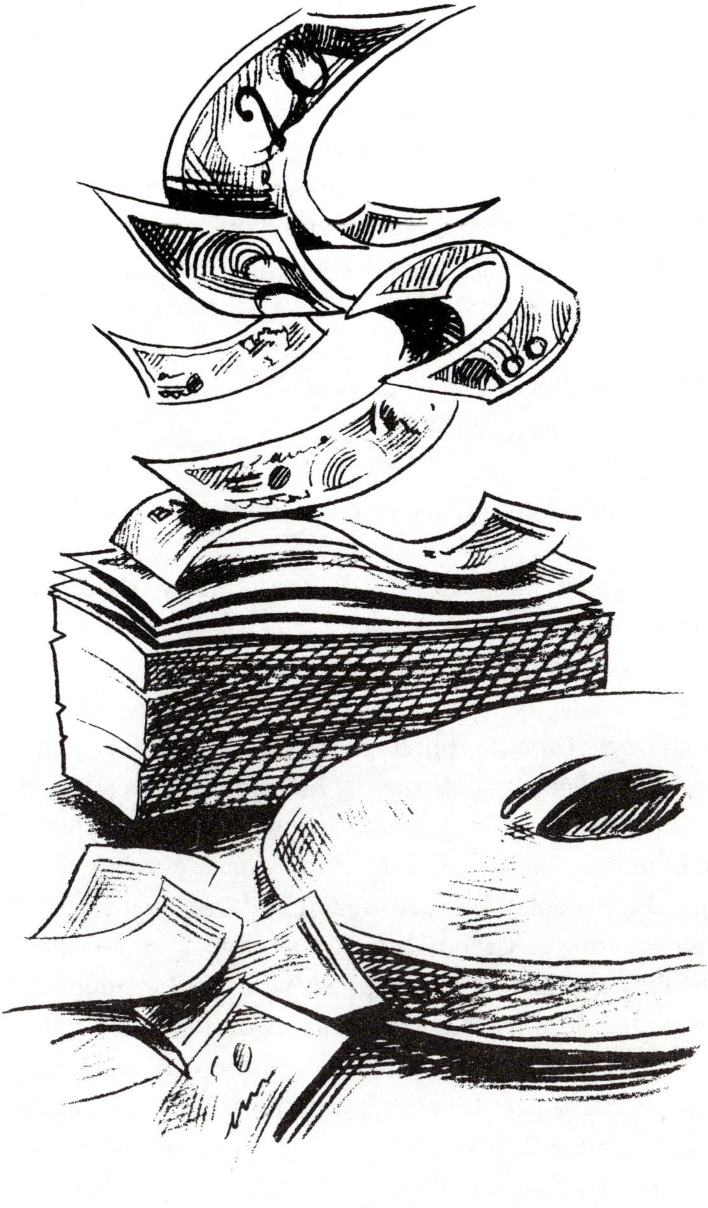

We put our curse on you. You will be an unhappy man for rejecting us. Don't you know that money can buy everything this world can offer? Money opens the door to pleasure, prestige and power. If you possess us, you will never lack anything which human beings long for. Money makes for happiness. Don't be a fool. Pick us up and take us home with you.'

Johnny replied, 'You are right, in a way. Money can indeed buy all the things this world can offer, yet it cannot buy the deepest longings of a person's heart. My heart has always felt satisfied even although I have never had you.'

'You are a liar!' said the notes. 'What do you know of the world and its pleasures? Come on, tell us what we cannot buy for you!'

Johnny smiled calmly down at the notes in the dustbin.

'It is true that money could buy me a golden bed, but it could not buy the sound sleep I enjoy. Money can buy cosmetics, but it cannot buy my healthy complexion. Money can buy a luxurious house, but it cannot buy my happy home. Money can buy sex, but it cannot buy my loving marriage. Money can buy people, but it cannot buy my loyal friends. Money can buy books, but it cannot buy knowledge and wisdom. Money can buy extravagant clothes, but it cannot buy personal dignity. Money can buy occasional fun, but it cannot buy inner joy and peace. Money can even buy me an expensive funeral, but it cannot buy the happy death I hope to have.

'In other words, whatever is worthwhile, whatever is truly precious in life, you, money, cannot buy. You can only bluff your way into "clever" people's lives, persuading them to believe that you can give what is not yours to give. You are a cheat and a liar. Stay just where you are, for that is where you belong – in the dustbin.'

With that, Johnny went on his way, whistling happily to himself.

QUESTIONS FOR DISCUSSION

1. If money cannot buy the most precious things in life, what drives people's cravings for wealth?

2. Do you think that rich people are happier than those who have just enough for their needs?

3. Is money good or bad? What is the true value of money?

4. Why did Jesus say that it will be hard for a rich man to enter the Kingdom of Heaven?

5. We are surrounded by advertisements and propaganda urging us to make money and to spend it. What do you think such a culture does to society?

6. What do you think the Gospels tell us about Jesus's attitude towards money and wealth?

POINTS FOR REFLECTION

1. Gandhi said, 'The world has enough for every man's need, but not enough for every man's greed.'

2. It is better to have a high standard of life than a high standard of living.

3. We must learn to possess money without being possessed by it. One measure of this is what we are willing to do to get it, and how willing we are to share it when we have it.

4. It is what we are that matters, not what we have.

Who killed Pat Hudson?

'Who killed Pat Hudson?' shouted someone in the crowd. 'Tell me, who killed the boxer, Pat Hudson?'

The referee said, 'Not I, surely. Don't point any fingers at me. Of course, I could have stopped the fight in the eighth round and then Pat might not have died, but the public would have been upset. They came to see a good fight, and they would say I had cheated them. It's very sad that he died, but it wasn't my fault. I did nothing to Pat Hudson.'

The crowds who had come to see the fight and whose shouts and cheers had filled the stadium said, 'We are not to blame. It's such a shame that a fine boxer like Pat died. It is a great loss to the world of sport. We never wanted him to die, far from it. Nobody can say we killed him. We only came to watch the fight.'

Pat Hudson's manager said, 'It is extremely painful for me to speak about Pat's death. His wife and children have suffered a terrible loss. I took it for granted that he was in good shape physically. If he wasn't fit enough to fight, he should have said so. Regrettably, he made an error of judgement. I have a clear conscience. Nobody can hold me responsible for what happened.'

The men at the betting booth said, 'Pat's death has nothing whatsoever to do with us. We weren't in the audience, and we have never even met the man. He was such a promising boxer. It's a great pity that he died, but it's not our fault.'

The journalist said, 'Don't look at me. I am completely innocent. I was just there to report on the fight for the morning papers. I was only doing my job. Sadly, these things happen sometimes. Pat's time was up.'

The boxer who knocked him out said, 'I did not kill Pat. I am not a murderer. I am a respectable human being and a fair sportsman. It's true that I hit him, but I did everything according to the rules of the game. Nobody can blame me for what happened. This was not 'murder' or 'manslaughter'. I will always remember Pat, but I feel no guilt. Perhaps it was his destiny to die like this. It was the will of God.'

Again, a small voice was heard calling from the crowd. 'Then, who killed the boxer Pat Hudson? Can't anybody tell me who it was?'

*An adaptation from the script of
a Spanish audiovisual*

QUESTIONS FOR DISCUSSION

1. What is the central theme of this story?

2. Can you mention similar incidents which you know of – in your school or college, your place of work, your family, or in the society in which we live?

3. How do such situations arise? Who is responsible for the injustices and evils in society?

4. What are the ideologies, values and assumptions which contribute towards global injustice?

5. What can we do about it? Where should we begin?

6. Have you ever felt guilty in unjust situations?

7. Have you ever helped any victims of injustice?

8. Can you give examples of occasions or circumstances where you feel that you yourself are a victim of social injustice?

9. When in trouble, have you ever felt betrayed or let down by your friends? What did you expect them to do for you?

POINTS FOR REFLECTION

1. We are part and parcel of the unjust systems which govern our world.

2. Often we are tempted to close our eyes to social problems and to invent reasonable-sounding excuses to justify our apathy. This is particularly tempting when we are the beneficiaries rather than the victims of injustice. Most people living in so-called First World countries benefit in some way from global injustice.

3. In seeking to build a just society, we must start with our personal relationships in family, school and work, but we must not end there. We are also responsible for wider issues of justice.

4. Democracy and freedom of speech bring responsibilities as well as rights and privileges. We share responsibility for the laws which are made and the policies which are pursued in our name.

The world map jigsaw puzzle

A child was told to piece together a jumbo jigsaw puzzle of the world map.

However hard he tried, he could not do the jigsaw. Then his mother gave him a clue.

'Look on the back of the puzzle pieces,' she said. 'There, you will find the drawing of a lifesize man, woman and child. Try putting them together first.'

The child did as his mother suggested, and sure enough, the jigsaw became much easier. As he fitted the pieces together, the picture of an attractive, smiling man and woman appeared, with a child between them.

He turned the jigsaw over very carefully, and there on the other side was the world map in perfect order.

QUESTIONS FOR DISCUSSION

1. When we look around we see so many divisions and factions. How might we begin to rebuild the broken picture of our world?

2. What is the first step towards global peace and harmony?

3. Can the world's systems – economic, social, political, religious, cultural – be put in order without considering human beings?

4. What did Christ come to change – the heart of mankind or the structures of the world?

5. If we want to create a better world, what must we focus on – ideologies or people?

6. 'The Word was made flesh.' What does this tell us about truth and the human experience?

7. What do we mean when we speak of 'structural sin'?

POINTS FOR REFLECTION

1. People are not made to serve the economy, the nation, politics, religion, culture or tradition. Rather, all these things are made to serve people. This helps us to see them in their true perspective.

2. All systems which put ideology before human reality are bound to fail. Ideas must be tested against the truth of human experience before they can be trusted.

PART 3
Personal and psychological values

The bird and the well

There was once a bird with brilliant plumage and strong wings who spent her days soaring high above the treetops, delighting in her freedom.

One day she fell into a disused well. The well was dark and deep, but it was dry and the bird was unhurt. She fluttered down and down until she touched the bottom, and there she stayed, doing nothing to try to escape, wallowing in self-pity.

'I shall surely die down here,' she moaned. 'What a poor, unhappy bird I am. What have I done to deserve such a fate?'

The more she considered her plight, the more she became convinced that it was somebody else's fault that she was at the bottom of the well.

'It's not my fault. It's the fault of the stupid person who dug the well in the first place,' she said. 'Somebody should have put a cover over the top, and then I wouldn't have fallen in. Why didn't anybody warn me about the danger of flying too low over open wells? None of this is my fault.'

She began calling for help to passers-by. 'Help! Help! Heeellllppp! Please help me. Pleeeease get me out of here.'

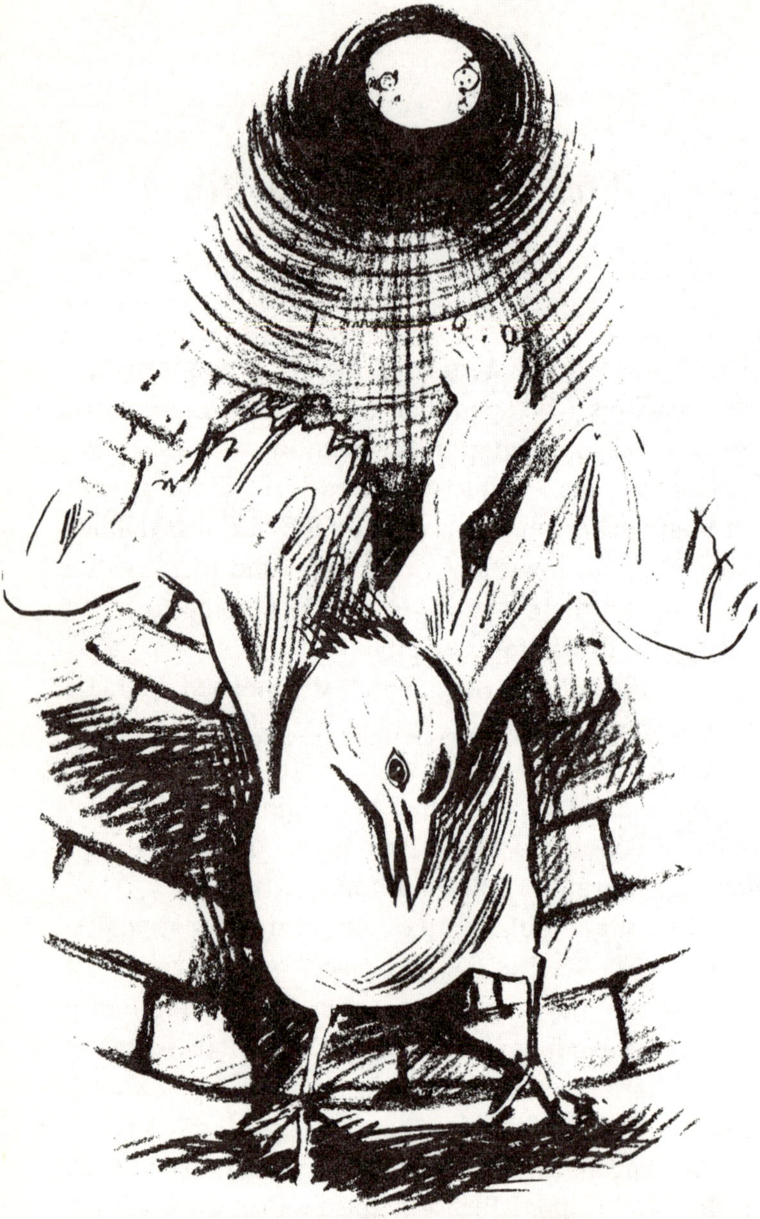

People stared into the well. 'You've got wings, you can fly,' they said. 'Why don't you help yourself?'

'If I try flying down here I might hurt myself,' the bird wailed. 'I might graze my wings against the walls of the well. It's not my fault I'm stuck down here. You've got to do something to get me out.'

The people called down to her, 'There's plenty of space to fly if you're careful. Your wings are fine. You're not hurt. You can escape if you really want to.'

The bird refused to try. She huddled on the bottom, grumbling and moaning to all who would listen.

'Nobody cares about me, that's the problem. People are so heartless and cruel, they're not interested in helping a poor suffering creature like me.'

The bird's complaints attracted so much sympathy that almost without realizing what was happening, she began to enjoy living in the well. She thought less and less about escaping, until it no longer occurred to her even to try. Her wings withered away, so that even had she wanted to fly to freedom, she would not have been able to. Now neither she nor anybody else could help her.

And so, pitied by all and pitying herself, the bird lived for the rest of her life trapped and miserable at the bottom of the well.

QUESTIONS FOR DISCUSSION

1. Why did the bird not try to fly out of the well?

2. How did she react when nobody came to rescue her?

3. Did the people outside do anything at all to help the bird?

4. Should they have done more?

5. Did the bird derive some benefit from staying where she was?

6. Do we ever behave this way – blaming others for our misfortunes and wallowing in self-pity? Can you think of examples?

POINTS FOR REFLECTION

1. Sometimes we risk being hurt if we try to be free. Often it feels more secure to be trapped.

2. There is a difference between being helped and being rescued. We may look to others for help and encouragement, but we can only rescue ourselves.

3. The desire to be pitied and to be the centre of attention can cripple us and prevent us from achieving our full potential.

The cuckoo

One day a young girl was walking in the woods when she heard a cuckoo. She looked up and saw the bird flying from branch to branch, singing joyfully.

'Cuckoo, won't you tell me where your house is?' asked the child.

The cuckoo replied: 'My house? The whole forest is my house.'

'My grandfather has a cuckoo at home,' said the girl. 'She lives in a little nest at the top of the clock and she never leaves the house. She doesn't keep singing all the time the way you do. She only sings once every hour.'

'Ah,' said the cuckoo. 'You mean a cuckoo that lives inside the clock and sings the time?'

'Yes, that's right,' said the girl. 'She's so pretty, and she sings beautifully.'

The cuckoo shook her head. 'That may be true, but she's not real.'

'What do you mean by real?' asked the child.

Patiently, the cuckoo explained. 'She cannot fly like me whenever she wants to. She has no friends. She cannot lay eggs. She cannot love, nor can she suffer. Her song is monotonous, with no feeling in it.'

The little girl was puzzled. 'But isn't it lovely to have a cosy little house, to sing every hour and to be cared for and prized by people?'

'Not at all,' replied the cuckoo. 'It's better to be free than to have a house, to sing whenever one wants to and not just on the hour, to care for others rather than to be cared for, to be loved instead of being prized.'

'I like you, cuckoo,' said the child. 'I love you. Please come to my house and sing for me every hour. I'll give you somewhere to stay. I'll be your friend, and you will be my friend.'

The cuckoo said, 'If you're really my friend, and if you love me, then don't take my freedom away. Allow me to be myself. If you love me and want to be my friend, then I will come to your garden to sing for you. I'll come to see you and to tell you that I love you. My visits may not be regular, but be sure, my singing will be lovelier than the singing of the cuckoo in your clock, and my visits will give you greater joy than the dead presence of the cuckoo forever locked inside your house. Our friendship will be sweet, warm and loving.'

'You mean real?' said the child.

'Yes, it will be real,' replied the cuckoo.

QUESTIONS FOR DISCUSSION

1. What were the differences between the cuckoo in the clock and the cuckoo in the forest?

2. Why did the child expect all cuckoos to behave like the cuckoo in the clock?

3. Does the child's attitude say anything about our own attitudes to society and the people around us?

4. When we educate children, do we help them to be alive, natural and spontaneous, or do we teach them to obey rules and become model citizens?

5. Can true friendship and intimacy develop in an atmos-phere of regimentation and formality?

POINTS FOR REFLECTION

1. We all need freedom if we are to grow into real people who are fully alive.

2. A life which is shielded from pain and sorrow and risk is also deprived of freedom and the full joy of living.

3. True love allows spontaneity and freedom in the way it is given and the way it is received.

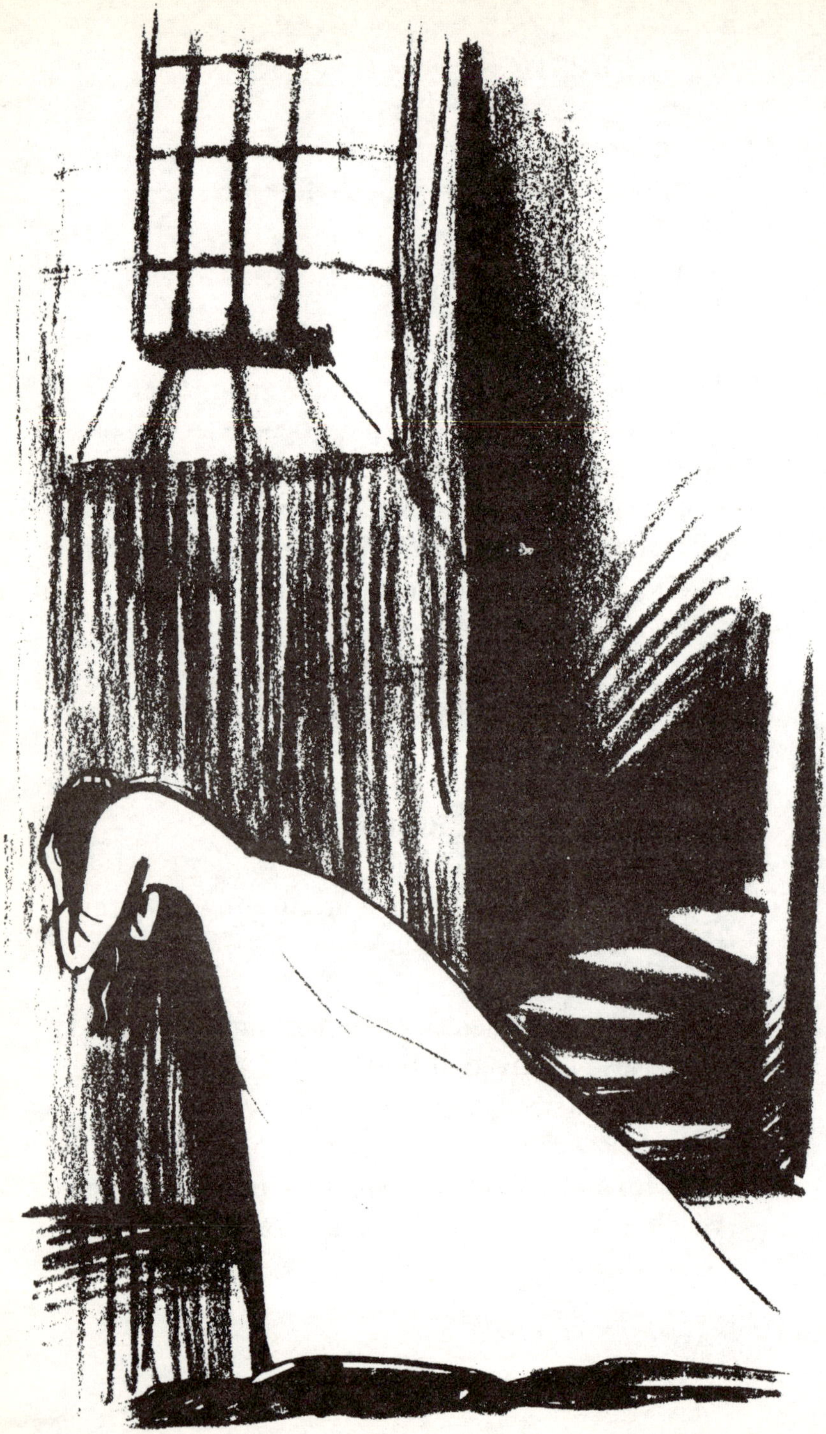

Princess Ugly

Once upon a time there was a beautiful princess. She was the most beautiful girl in the world. Her stepmother was jealous of the princess's beauty, and from the earliest days of her childhood she kept telling her,

'You are ugly! You are very, very ugly! You are so ugly that people can't bear to look at you.' Not only that, but she gave orders to all the courtiers in the palace to say the same, so that everybody the princess met told her how ugly she was.

The princess grew into a beautiful woman, but she was in despair.

'I am ugly,' she wept to herself. 'I am so ugly that nobody will ever like me. Nobody will ever love me. Nobody will ever want to marry me.'

Finally, her sorrow was so great that she hid herself in the palace dungeons so that nobody would ever have to look at her again. There she stayed, alone and hating herself because she believed she was so ugly.

When the queen died, some kindhearted people in the palace went to see the princess.

'Your stepmother hated you, but she's dead now,'

they said. 'What she told you was a lie. You are not ugly. You are very beautiful. You are the most beautiful girl we have ever seen.'

The princess refused to believe them. 'I know that's not true. Can't you see how ugly I am? Please, leave me alone to die in my grief and ugliness.'

One day, a handsome prince visited the palace and people told him about the princess living in the dungeon. He went down to find her, and as soon as he saw her he was enthralled.

'You are lovely,' he said. 'You are so beautiful, so very beautiful, I cannot take my eyes off you.'

The princess covered her face with her hands and cried.

'Please go away!' she said. 'I know how ugly I am. Please, stop taunting me and leave me alone. I am the ugliest girl in the world. I know I am.'

But the prince would not go. He came closer to her, captivated by her beauty.

'You are beautiful,' he murmured. 'You are very, very beautiful.'

'No! No! Why are you doing this to me?' the princess wailed. 'Please, don't torment me like this. Go away, I beg you.'

The prince put his arms around her and gazed down at her. 'You're beautiful,' he whispered. 'You are the most beautiful woman in the world.'

At last, hearing the love and tenderness in his voice, the princess raised her eyes to his. There, reflected in her lover's eyes, she saw her own image for the very first time. She felt confused, and then astonished. She looked intently at the face reflected in his pupils, and slowly it dawned on her that the beautiful face she saw there was her own. She laughed in wonderment and joy.

'I am beautiful,' she said. 'I really am beautiful.'

QUESTIONS FOR DISCUSSION

1. What did the queen hope to achieve by telling the princess she was ugly?

2. Why was the princess so full of self-loathing and despair?

3. Why did the princess refuse to believe those who told her she was beautiful?

4. How did the prince persuade her of her beauty?

5. What do we mean by self-image?

6. What influence does our self-image have on the way we feel about ourselves and on the way we behave towards others?

7. Which is more likely to make us open and trusting towards others – a positive self-image or a negative one?

8. Can you apply this story to everyday life? What does it say about the way we treat people in personal relationships and in society?

POINTS FOR REFLECTION

1. People are like psychological mirrors for one another. Positive feedback, acceptance and love build up a positive self-image. Negative feedback, destructive criticism and rejection build up a negative self-image.

2. When the princess perceived herself to be ugly in the eyes of others, she began to believe that she was ugly and this affected her behaviour towards others.

3. The princess's negative self-image was deeply ingrained. It was only by patience and loving persistence that the prince persuaded her to see her true image reflected in his eyes.

4. To bring out the beauty in another person, we need to recognise and acknowledge that person's worth.

Proscrustes

High in the mountains in the country of Attica in ancient Greece, there lived a strange man by the name of Procrustes.

Procrustes used to lie in wait beside the mountain passes which were common in that hilly region, and ambush unsuspecting travellers on their journeys. Not only did he make his living by robbing people, but he also devised a way of making his work entertaining as well as lucrative. He made an iron bed exactly to his own dimensions, and whenever he had robbed a passer-by he made the hapless victim lie stretched out upon his bed. If by chance his 'client' fitted perfectly, Procrustes was delighted and would refund all he had stolen. But woe to the poor 'client' who did not fit exactly into the bed.

If the person was too small, Procrustes would pound him with a mallet, flattening him out until he filled the bed. If he was too big, then Procrustes would set about amputating whichever limbs were necessary to make the 'client' fit the bed.

This sport made Procrustes feel exceedingly important and pleased with himself.

A Greek legend

QUESTIONS FOR DISCUSSION

1. What must we do to people if we expect them to behave in a uniform way?

2. Can we measure others according to our own beliefs and expectations?

3. What happens when teachers, parents and those in authority treat people as numbers rather than as individuals?

POINTS FOR REFLECTION

1. Each person is his or her own measure.

2. It is our right to be, and our duty to let others be.

3. In order to achieve uniformity, we cripple, torture and destroy others.

4. Each of us is bound by our own conscience. We cannot judge others, only ourselves.

5. There is beauty in diversity.

6. Ideologies – political, cultural and religious – more often than not are Procrustean beds.

Which guide to follow?

A traveller had to journey on foot across a formidable mountain range. He did not know the way and he was afraid.

He managed to obtain a detailed map of the region which clearly showed all the roads and tracks and footpaths. He said to himself, 'This map will be useful, but if I could travel with a local guide, somebody who knows the way by heart, I would feel even more confident.'

As luck would have it, the traveller met a local inhabitant who was travelling to the same destination and was very familiar with the route. The men set out together, walking side by side. Our traveller carried his map and checked every twist and turn they made, and he was pleased to discover that his companion was keeping exactly to the route marked out on the map.

Suddenly, to the traveller's alarm, his guide turned down an unmarked path.

'My friend, why are you going this way?' he asked. 'This path is not shown on my map, and I'm afraid to follow you. Do you want us both to get lost and perish among the mountains?'

His companion explained, 'What you do not know is that the path shown on your map was recently destroyed by a landslide and is no longer usable. Don't worry. Trust me rather than your map. I will show you another path if you follow me.'

The traveller refused. 'No, I will not follow you! How can you tell me to follow you along a route which is not marked? I feel much safer sticking to the paths which my map tells me to use.'

'Trust me, my friend,' said the guide. 'I have known these mountains all my life. I was born here and I grew up here. I know where I am going. You will be safe if you follow me.'

But the traveller would not be persuaded. 'I'm sorry, but if you insist on taking a different path I will go my own way. I prefer to trust my map than to take your word for it.'

The traveller and his companion parted company. The traveller journeyed on with his map in his hand, while the other let experience be his guide. The local inhabitant reached his destination. As for our traveller, nobody knows what happened to him.

QUESTIONS FOR DISCUSSION

1. What do you think happened to the traveller and why?

2. What are the dangers of being a stickler for rules and regulations?

3. Who would you rather trust – a learned person or an experienced person? Why?

4. What is better – academic knowledge or experiential knowledge? Why?

5. On our journey to God, what is more helpful – a good book or a good guide?

6. Why do we find it hard to entrust ourselves to an experienced guide?

7. Are there any other lessons which you can find in the story?

POINTS FOR REFLECTION

1. To be a good guide we must have experienced what we teach.

2. Somebody had to walk over the mountains in order to draw the map.

3. Academic knowledge is good, but it is not enough. Rules and norms should be our guides, not our masters.

4. We only really know that which we ourselves have experienced.

5. Rational, linear thinking is not sufficient for every situation in life. We also need to trust our experiences, intuitions and inspirations.

6. It is hard to allow oneself to be guided by another, for there is the fear of having to surrender one's control to someone else.

The portrait

Sidney Smith was something of a celebrity in the town where he lived. One day he decided to commission a local artist to paint his portrait. The artist did a preliminary sketch and showed it to Sidney for his approval. It was a perfect likeness, but Sidney was outraged.

'This isn't what I wanted at all!' he said. 'You've made my face look too round. You'll have to do it again.'

The painter did another sketch, but still Sidney wasn't satisfied.

'My shoulders don't look broad enough,' he said. 'Do it again, but this time do something about the shoulders.'

The artist did another sketch with a thinner face and broader shoulders.

Sidney shook his head impatiently. 'It's still not right,' he said. 'I think the shape of the chin is wrong, and the eyes are too small. I don't like the nose either.'

The painter did sketch after sketch, until finally Sidney was happy.

'Good,' he said. 'At last I'm beginning to like myself.'

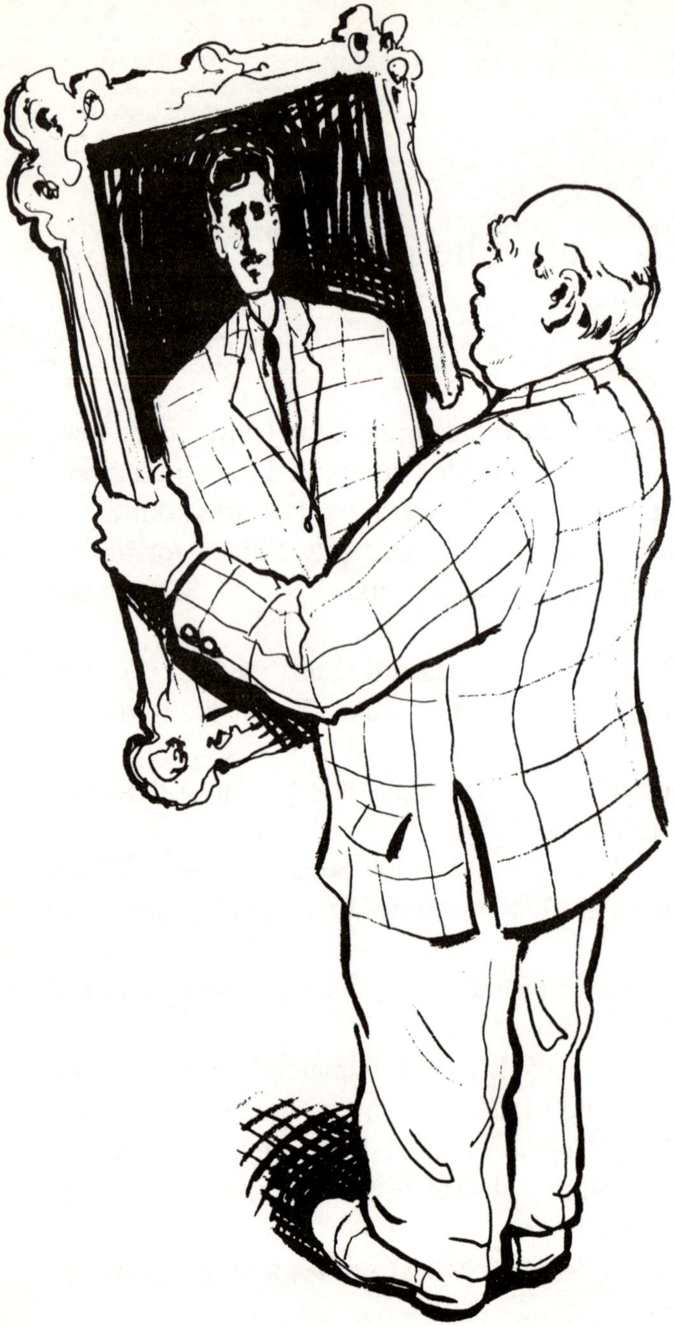

When he took the portrait home, he invited all his friends and relations to come and see it. Everybody burst out laughing.

'What a dreadful artist!' they said. 'That doesn't look a bit like you. How could he portray you like that? He hasn't captured any of your qualities – the kindness of your face, the twinkle in your eyes. We think you look much nicer as you really are.'

When they'd all gone, Sidney looked at the picture in shame and embarassment. He wrapped it in brown paper and took it back to the artist.

'I've changed my mind,' he said. 'I'd like you to do the portrait again, but this time make it like the original sketch you showed me. I've decided that's the one I like best.'

QUESTIONS FOR DISCUSSION

1. Why didn't Sidney like the first sketch?

2. What was Sidney really rejecting – the sketch or himself?

3. When Sidney said, 'At last I'm beginning to like myself,' was he being honest? When did he begin to like himself?

4. Why didn't his friends and family like the portrait?

5. What does this story tell us about our self-image?

POINTS FOR REFLECTION

1. Sometimes our ideal self is very different from our real self. We need to learn to see ourselves and accept ourselves as we really are.
2. Those close to us love us for who we are not for who we think we'd like to be.

3. A poor self-image can distort the way we present ourselves to others. We need to trust people to accept us as we really are.

Tom and Sam

There were once two dogs called Tom and Sam. One day, the dogs were walking in the woods. It was hot and they were thirsty, so they were delighted when they discovered a clear, sparkling pond. They rushed to the water's edge and bent down to drink, but what a fright they had! There, staring back at them, were two of the scruffiest, ugliest dogs they had ever seen.

Tom hated the reflection that stared up at him. In disgust and loathing, he ran away as fast as he could, but his flight was in vain. Wherever he went, the detested image stared back at him from every polished surface, from every puddle and pond, from every mirror. His life was wasted on the futile endeavour of trying to get away from his own reflection.

What about Sam? His reaction was rather different from Tom's.

When Sam saw the image in the pond, he also hated it. His immediate reaction was to destroy it. He snarled, and the dog snarled back at him. In a fury, Sam jumped into the water to tear the other dog to pieces, but the dog disappeared. Disappointed and wet, he dragged himself out of the pond and lay down in the sun to dry off. After a while he looked into the pond again, and to his astonishment the other dog had reappeared. Wild with rage, he jumped into the pond again, more determined than ever to destroy his enemy, but once again it disappeared.

Everywhere Sam went, he saw the other dog and tried to attack it. He threw himself, snarling and biting, at every mirror, every polished surface, into every pond and puddle, but all in vain. His life became a useless, painful struggle to destroy the elusive dog which appeared in front of him wherever he went.

QUESTIONS FOR DISCUSSION

1. What do the reflections in the pond represent?

2. Does this story tell us anything about what really happens in many people's lives?

3. Why did Tom keep running away from his reflection? Why was it impossible for him to escape?

4. Why do people often feel withdrawn and lonely?

5. What might Tom have done to live a contented life?

6. Why did Sam attack his reflection? Was it possible for him to destroy it?

7. Does Sam's story help us to understand people who seem aggressive and angry?

8. What might Sam have done to live a peaceful life?

POINTS FOR REFLECTION

1. Most of us find it difficult to like ourselves as we are. We refuse to accept ourselves, even to the point of hating ourselves.

2. If we are unable to love and accept ourselves, we cannot love and accept others.

3. If we dislike ourselves and others, we will never be able to face reality but will choose between *flight* and *fight*.

    The *flight reaction* leads us to run away from ourselves and others. When we run away from the reality of human life we suffer withdrawal, shyness, loneliness, discouragement, boredom and a sense of futility.

    The *fight reaction* makes us fight reality, even to the extent of destroying ourselves and others. This continuous need to fight results in condemnation of self and others, back-biting, resentment, intolerance, bitterness, anger and misery.

4. The only way out of this struggle is to accept and love reality. We need to accept ourselves as we are, to love ourselves as God made us, and to know that God loves each and every human being with absolute, unconditional love.

To save or not to save one's skin

Many years ago, all the animals lived in peace together in the forest. One unhappy day, a man arrived in the forest carrying a strange instrument and he killed a deer. The next day he returned and killed a tiger. From that time on, man continued to kill, capture and cage the animals, one after another, until finally they called a meeting among themselves to discuss how to defend themselves against man's cruelty.

The elephant spoke first because he was much bigger and more imposing than any of the other creatures. 'My tactic is to scare people,' he said. 'When I see humans, I charge towards them with my ears flapping and my great tusks raised in warning, trampling everything in my path and making the earth tremble.'

The tiger spoke after the elephant. 'I believe that attack is the best form of defence,' she roared. 'Before a man knows what is happening, I creep up and spring on him, and I use my powerful jaws and sharp claws to defend myself.'

Next, the deer spoke in a timid whisper. 'My security lies in the speed with which I can run. Whenever I catch the smell of man, I run like the wind until I am out of sight. That way, he can never catch me.'

'I detest man,' hissed the snake. My method is the most cunning of all. I lie hidden in the grass, and I am happy to stay there, quiet and still, for hours on end. Whenever man approaches, my heart cries out for revenge and I bite him, sinking my poisonous fangs into his flesh and delighting in the pain I cause him.'

The tortoise blinked sleepily. 'My method is very simple,' she said. 'I just withdraw until the danger passes. I have built myself a thick, protective shell which I always carry on my back. At the first sight of a human being, I hide inside my shell where I can see nothing and hear nothing. I feel very secure in there.'

The dog wagged his tail and smiled. 'Friends, if you will bear with me for a moment, I will tell you why I think you are all wrong. We have to accept that human beings are here to stay, and they are far superior to us. They are a great threat to us, and it is foolish to believe that we can fight them or scare them or run away from them or destroy them. For our own sakes, let's learn to obey them, to become their allies and friends. I've decided to allow myself to become domesticated by people. I will stay in their homes and serve them, and although I might lose my freedom, at least I will be assured of a warm place to sleep, food and peace of mind. We must be practical about these things, my friends.'

The chameleon spoke last of all. She raised her head and haughtily surveyed the creatures around her. 'What fools you are, with all this talk about frightening them, attacking them, running away, befriending them. You don't need to do any of those things if you adopt my method. I just keep changing my colour to suit the occasion. I don't mind how often I have to change. It doesn't bother me what I look like or how many identities I have. The only thing that really matters is whether or not you want to save your skin.'

QUESTIONS FOR DISCUSSION

1. What is the purpose of this story? Can you explain it?

2. What do you think of the attitudes adopted by the various animals? Were they helpful? Honest? Reasonable?

3. Consider some human responses which reflect the same attitudes as the animals' responses (for example, aggression, escapism, duplicity, self-deception, servility, opportunism, etc.).

4. What do you think is the best attitude to take when being criticised, attacked or threatened?

5. Would you identify with any particular animal in the story? Why?

6. Is there a conflict facing you at the present time? If you are willing to share it, perhaps you could say how you have dealt with it so far, and what you might do about it from now on.

POINTS FOR REFLECTION

1. Sooner or later, we are all faced with difficulties, opposition and conflict. Different people opt for different strategies to deal with these challenges. Some strategies are more honest and constructive than others.

2. It is not possible to apply a single strategy to every situation. Each new challenge may demand a different approach, yet whatever approach we take we should aim to be constructive, dignified, compassionate and rational.

3. The two important elements in responding to any difficult situation are assertiveness and self-esteem. By assertiveness we mean the will always to have one's rights respected, while at the same time respecting the rights of others. By self-esteem we mean never being willing to do ourselves something we would not respect others for doing.

The unbeaten road

Hidden among the mountains in a far off country there was a village. At the entrance to the village there were three roads, and where the roads branched away from each other there were three signs. One read, 'To the sea', the other, 'To the city', and the third, 'To nowhere'.

From as far back as anybody could remember, people had only ever travelled along the first two roads. Nobody had ever dared to go along the road that led 'to nowhere'. It remained deserted and untravelled.

Jane, a child in the village, kept asking the villagers the same question: 'Where does the road that leads to nowhere go?' Invariably, she was given the same reply: 'Nowhere'.

The villagers were afraid for the little girl's safety and they told her, 'Don't ever go along that road. It's very dangerous. No one has ever had the courage to travel along it.' But Jane thought to herself, 'If there's a road, it must lead somewhere!'

One day, Jane slipped away from the village and made her way stealthily along the forbidden road. She travelled for a long, long way, over hills and valleys, past streams and waterfalls, through forests and deserts.

On and on she went, until she began to think that the villagers had been right. The road really did lead to nowhere.

Then one day she spotted a dog, and she said to herself, 'If there's a dog, there must be a house or at least a person nearby.'

With a mixture of fear and hope, she followed the dog. It led her down a path to a house hidden away in a leafy grove. An old woman lived in the house. Who was she? A fairy perhaps, or a kindly spirit? Nobody knows.

'Come, little girl,' she said to Jane. 'Come into my house. It is beautiful and full of treasures. For many, many years I have been waiting for someone to visit me.'

She showed Jane her mansion filled with rare and precious treasures. 'Take anything you want, child,' she said. 'Anything I possess is yours for the asking. It is your reward for having the courage to travel along the road that led to nowhere. For all these years I have waited, but nobody has ever dared to make the journey before.'

Laden with gold and jewels, Jane said goodbye to the kind old woman. The dog led her back to the road and she returned to the village.

The villagers meanwhile suspected that Jane had disobeyed them and travelled along the forbidden road. Anxious and fretful, they were convinced that some terrible fate had befallen her and they would never see her again. They were astonished when they saw her travelling towards them along the road, carrying her precious load of treasure. Trustingly, she told them the truth about her journey, and they listened in wonder and amazement.

Soon there was a rush of villagers embarking upon the road to nowhere, greedy for the rewards which awaited them. For days and nights they walked, never stopping to rest, until they reached nowhere. They could not find the little dog, nor the house, nor the kind old woman.

They returned to the village full of bitterness and disappointment, cursing Jane and accusing her of being a liar and a cheat.

Jane shook her head and said quietly, 'It is true there is treasure to be found, but only for those who dare to travel along a road that leads to nowhere.'

An adaptation of a fable by Gianni Rodari

QUESTIONS FOR DISCUSSION

1. Why had nobody before Jane dared to travel along the road to nowhere?

2. What sort of person does Jane represent?

3. What do the treasures found by Jane symbolise?

4. Who do the villagers rushing after Jane typify? Who are they in real life?

5. Why did only Jane find the treasure?

6. Would humankind have progressed at all if nobody had ever dared to enter a road that led to nowhere? Why?
7. Why have pioneers and visionaries always been branded as crazy and rash?
8. Are you like Jane or are you like the other villagers? Why?

POINTS FOR REFLECTION

1. There are no gains without risks.

2. Nobody who dares to take a road that is said to lead to nowhere can be called a failure. The real failures are those who are not willing to try the road at all.

3. When a pioneer succeeds, he or she is remembered as a discoverer or an inventor. Those who do not succeed are remembered as fools and failures by those who do not themselves dare to journey along untravelled roads.

The tree, the roots and the soil

In the middle of the forest stood a huge tree, the most magnificent tree for miles around. One day, the roots addressed themselves to the tree.

'It is a fact that everybody who sees you admires your majesty and your beauty. You have the glossiest leaves, the finest flowers, the sweetest fruit of all the trees in the forest. You are rightly praised for your splendour, because you are the greatest of all the trees. But have you ever thought of us, your roots? Although nobody sees us or praises us, we give you the strength to hold your head high above your fellow trees. We are shapeless and without beauty, yet we are responsible for your magnificence. We have no perfume of our own, yet we supply the fragrance you exude from your richly coloured flowers. Although we seem barren, we provide you with sap to produce your abundant fruits. In other words, everything you are is ours, dear tree, for a tree is only as good as its roots.'

At this, the soil interrupted. 'My dear tree and my dear roots, do you not realize that it is the soil – the least acknowledged and the least praised – which in truth gives you all that you have, and makes you what you are. Without me, there would be neither tree nor roots. I sustain both in my loving arms. In my embrace you find nourishment, security and strength. I am the one who holds you firm. I give you water and vitality. All of you, roots, trunk, branches, leaves, flowers and fruits are born from me. Everything you are derives its quality from me, the soil.'

QUESTIONS FOR DISCUSSION

1. What sort of tree are you? Consider the fruits and flowers you produce, your achievements and successes, your weaknesses and failures.

2. What sort of roots do you have – family and friends, education, significant people in your life? Do your roots nourish you or deplete you? Do you make full use of the insights, skills and learning which you acquire from your roots?

3. What influence have your roots had on you, especially on your personality and behaviour?

4. Have you ever thanked those people in whom your life is rooted?

5. Consider the soil in which you grow – your social environment, cultural background, economic class and religious affiliation. How have these influenced you and helped you to become what you are?

6. From where do you derive your values, ideals, goals and ambitions?

7. Are you happy being the tree you are? Is there anything you want to change? How can you bring about change?

POINTS FOR REFLECTION

1. 'No man is an island.' This well-known saying reflects the fact that we are dependent on one another, on our family, our culture and our society, to provide an environment in which we can flourish and grow.

2. There is no such thing as a self-made person. We are shaped by the circumstances of our lives.

3. For change to be effective, we must work to change the soil in which we are rooted. It is not enough just to change our outward appearances.

by the same author:
PARABLES AND FABLES FOR MODERN MAN

Parables encompass the depth and breadth of human existence and reflect the meaning of life through images and symbols. Jesus himself, by "speaking in parables", touched the lives of people and opened before their eyes the treasures of the kingdom.

Presented in this book are thirty fascinating stories bearing on a variety of topics of interest to modern man, with commentaries and bible references to help the reader appreciate the thrust of each story and its application to actual life-situations. Besides providing a wholesome reading to those with a "flight of fancy", this book is an invaluable help especially for teachers and group leaders, to encourage active discussion and the sharing of ideas.

085439 325 0   £5.95